The Mystery of Samba

A BOOK IN THE SERIES

Latin America
in Translation /
en Traducción /
em Tradução

Sponsored by the Duke–University of North Carolina

Joint Program in Latin American Studies

THE MYSTERY OF

SAMBA

Popular Music & National Identity in Brazil

HERMANO VIANNA

Edited and Translated by JOHN CHARLES CHASTEEN

The University of North Carolina Press Chapel Hill & London

Originally published in Portuguese with
the title O mistério do samba (Rio de Janeiro:
J. Zahar Editor and the Universidade Federal
do Rio de Janeiro, 1995).
Designed by Richard Hendel
Set in Quadraat and Matra
by Tseng Information Systems, Inc.
Manufactured in the United States of America
Translation of the books in the series Latin America
in Translation / en Traducción / em Tradução, a
collaboration between the Duke–University of
North Carolina Joint Program in Latin American
Studies and the university presses of Duke and the
University of North Carolina, is supported by a
grant from the Andrew W. Mellon Foundation.
The paper in this book meets the guidelines for
permanence and durability of the Committee on
Production Guidelines for Book Longevity of the
Council on Library Resources.
Library of Congress Cataloging-in-Publication Data
Vianna, Hermano, 1960–
[Mistério do samba. English]
The mystery of samba : popular music and national
identity in Brazil / by Hermano Vianna ; edited and
translated by John Charles Chasteen.
     p.   cm. — (Latin America in translation/en
traducción/em tradução)
Includes bibliographical references and index.
ISBN 0-8078-2464-x (cloth : alk. paper). —
ISBN 0-8078-4766-6 (pbk. : alk. paper)
1. Samba (Dance)—Brazil.   2. Popular music—
Brazil—History and criticism.   3. Music and society—
Brazil.   I. Chasteen, John Charles, 1955–
II. Title.   III. Series.
ML3465.V5313   1999
784.18'88—dc21   98-22170
                    CIP
                    MN

03   5   4   3

For
Herbert and Helder,
my brothers, who lend
continuity (onstage and
backstage) to the history
of Brazilian music

We never finish arriving,
the moving island and I.
Mobile earth, uncertain sky,
world never discovered.

—*Jorge de Lima*

It's nothing like they say.
Samba moved to the favelas later on.
Anyway, it went wherever we went:
Wherever there was a party!

—*Donga*

CONTENTS

Translator's Preface

Samba is Brazil's "national rhythm," its prime symbol of cultural nationalism. Samba is also the centerpiece of Rio's world-famous pre-Lenten carnival, when samba dancers, who are predominantly black, from the city's poor neighborhoods parade all night under the glare of sophisticated all-night telemedia, broadcast nationwide.

To the outsider, samba and carnival seem to showcase Brazil's African heritage. Within Brazil, however, they stand for mixture— *mestiçagem*, racial and cultural mixture. Since the 1930s, Brazilians have, overall, enthusiastically adopted the notion that racial and cultural mixture define their unique national identity. Samba is the great metaphor for the mixture. Brazilians without a trace of African ancestry proudly claim "something African" in their sensibility.

How did Brazil become "the Kingdom of Samba" only a few decades after abolishing slavery in 1888? Anthropologist Hermano Vianna shows that samba traditions were invented through complex cultural mediations. This postmodern approach sets Vianna's work apart from most writing on samba. For Vianna, "authenticity" is always a social construction. Meanwhile, "authenticity" is the holy grail of most samba research: the authentic location of samba's birthplace, the authentic samba instrumentation, the authentic identities of its creators.

When I first met Hermano in 1994, he invited me to join him while he filmed some "old guard" samba players (*sambistas*) for Brazilian television. We drove to a clubhouse in the poor northern neighborhoods of Rio de Janeiro where, after everyone enjoyed an unhurried black bean feast, the old guard sambistas were interviewed and then showed their stuff for the cameras. Their stuff was old-fashioned, lightly tripping, string-driven samba, delivered with seemingly effortless pleasure—although some venerable dancers, too wise to attempt the normally lightning-fast steps, compensated with expressive grace what they lacked in speed. The young, hip film crew watched with quiet respect. Then the musicians were joined by Marisa Monte, a top singer of Brazilian popular music, who had recently recorded some sambas but was in no sense a traditional sambista. Hermano, who had created this show for Brazilian television, seemed particularly interested—even a touch apprehensive—when Marisa Monte sang English lyrics to a traditional samba accompaniment. The song, Lou Reed's "Pale Blue Eyes," was untraditional, indeed. If Hermano worried about the veteran sambistas' reaction, though, he need not have. Their smiles remained relaxed and gracious as they played on. Only later, after reading *The Mystery of Samba*, did I fully appreciate the moment.

The cultural politics surrounding samba signal its continued symbolic importance. Traditional samba is not played much on Brazilian radio anymore except at carnival time. The closest often-played popular genre would be pagode (or suingue), which, the purists would insist, is not *really* samba. Ordinarily, most Brazilians prefer listening to various genres of Brazilian popular music—including homegrown rock, country, funk, blues, and new dance music from Bahia, the capital of Afro-Brazil—as well as music from the United States. But nothing has so far threatened to replace samba as Brazil's "national rhythm," and a great deal is invested in its purity and authenticity.

Hermano Vianna, on the other hand, personally revels in cultural hybridity. His first book was about Brazilian funk. One might logically anticipate iconoclasm in his study of samba, but Vianna is not gleefully smashing icons here. Like the earlier Brazilian intellectuals who appear in his pages, Vianna lives (and travels) in an international world of ideas: hence, "the invention of tradition." Nevertheless, his loyalties are Brazilian. And nothing (except maybe soccer) has made more Brazilians proud of their country than samba, symbolizing, as it does, the hopeful fiction that Brazil has transcended race prejudice. Vianna does not believe the fiction. But he does not scorn it, either.

Scorn for official platitudes about Brazilian "racial democracy" has animated a number of recent U.S. multiculturalist views. They emphasize that, when racial and cultural mixing becomes a nationalist ideology, other racial identities (especially indigenous and African ones) remain marginalized and may be snuffed out altogether. In Brazil, the multiculturalist critique has circulated only in narrow intellectual circles and seems unlikely, for now, to diminish the popular appeal of mixed-race (mestiço) nationalism. After all, it was not so long ago—in the 1930s—that mestiço nationalism overthrew and replaced the official doctrines of white supremacy. Nor is white supremacy gone from Brazil, except officially. Therefore, the basic nationalist message—"It's okay not to be white and European"—retains its value in many people's lives. The mestiço category is so loose as to exclude almost nobody who seeks an "authentic Brazilian" identity.

In *The Mystery of Samba*, an English-speaking audience will encounter Brazil's century-old intellectual conversation on race, popular culture, and national identity. Because Vianna reviews its highlights so accessibly and ruminates on its future so open-endedly, *The Mystery of Samba* provides an excellent introduction to that conversation. But Vianna is not an impartial outsider. This book is itself part of this conversation overheard, and its author is, in some respects a modern (postmodern?) counterpart of the public intellectuals whom he studies. *The Mystery of Samba* is not a reply to U.S. multiculturalists. Nor does it speak internationally in scholarly jargon, anthropologist to anthropologist. For the most part, this anthropologist (who today works in television) is addressing Brazilians about Brazil. The text under explication is "the story that Brazilians once so liked to tell themselves about themselves: *Once upon a time we discovered the pride of living in a mestiço country where everything is mixed together.*"

Vianna wonders aloud, toward the end of his book, whether the "we" in that story remains meaningful. In the meantime, though, he uses the first-person plural inclusively and unselfconsciously to mean "we Brazilians." Somehow, with or without samba, globalization, multiculturalism, or mestiço nationalism, Brazilians seem safer from anomie than most people I know.

John Charles Chasteen
Chapel Hill, March 1998

Author's Preface to the U.S. Edition

This book is about the transformation of samba into Brazil's national music, a process that centered on Rio de Janeiro. The city of Rio has long been—and perhaps remains—utterly central to representations of Brazilian national unity. As a narrative and interpretive thread, I use the intellectual trajectory of anthropologist Gilberto Freyre (1900–1987), whose vast and controversial influence makes him, necessarily, a central figure of social thought in twentieth-century Brazil. Freyre's home was the Brazilian northeast, not Rio de Janeiro, but that does not matter. This book is about movement, about back-and-forth flows of influence that connected Rio not only to Pernambuco, but to France, the United States, and the rest of the Atlantic world as well. Various kinds of cultural mediation, spanning geographical and social distances, became crucial to the "nationalization" of samba. Freyre was one of the mediators.

Freyre was the ardent intellectual exponent of a unified Brazilian national culture, symbolized by samba and rooted in race mixing, or mestiçagem. My purpose is to argue neither for nor against Freyre's vision of "mestiço" nationalism. Instead, I take this ideology as an unavoidable fact of Brazilian life in the second half of the twentieth century and examine its genesis. How and why did Brazilian "authenticity" become essentially "Afro-Brazilian"? This proliferation of quotation marks suggests my emphasis on the social construction of our supposed cultural "essence."

The invention of Brazil's national essence, at least in the version symbolized by samba, turns on the importance of "popular culture." Popular culture tends to mean something different in the United States and in Brazil. David Riesman's pioneering 1950 article "Listening to Popular Music" loosely defines popular culture as "radio, movies, comics, popular music and fiction."[1] On the other hand, the Brazilian discourse on popular culture has either ignored radio and movies or considered them foreign, even hostile, terrain. Popular culture and "pop culture" have never blurred together in Brazilian studies. They have not been considered allied cultural forms, nor subjected to a similar analysis. Samba, despite its long and intense association with the Brazilian mass media, is never thought to have originated (or even really to belong) there. Pop culture has been viewed, to the contrary, as a corrupting, alienating influence: the worst enemy of "authentic" popular culture. During the 1960s, the radical defenders of Brazilian "authenticity" refused to accept pop culture diversions as "a valid method of communication with the masses," concluding that "only political art can be truly popular."[2] The defense of "authentic" popular culture in Brazil has often gained its energy from anti-U.S. cultural nationalism accompanied by revolutionary vision.

This book has its origins in my doctoral dissertation, defended at the Museu Nacional de Antropologia Social, Universidade Federal do Rio de Janeiro, in 1994. I am still surprised to have written a book about samba. That was not my interest when I began my doctorate in anthropology. To the contrary, my plan was to study the place of rock music — Brazilian rock, that is — in our national culture. But research on music and national identity in Brazil led me, inevitably, to samba, and I ended up (almost) totally seduced. The change in topic occurred during my stay at Northwestern University, in the United States, when I had the experience — trite but true — of observing Brazil from a distance. Never before had I felt so "Brazilian." The result was an exploration full of discoveries and surprises. The occasional tone of intellectual recklessness that I find upon rereading these pages for the English-language edition reflects the excitement with which they were written. I hope to share some of that excitement with the reader. My own initiation into the mystery of samba began when I happened to read of a little-known gathering that brought together two circles of friends — friends of Gilberto Freyre and friends of Pixinguinha, the famous samba player. The encounter took place in Rio de Janeiro in 1926.

Acknowledgments

he Italians say that translation equals treachery, but there are exceptions. John Chasteen's translation is simultaneously careful *and* creative, never treacherous. If anything, the English-language version of this book clarifies the ideas expressed originally in Portuguese.

Many others, too, have helped along the way. I gratefully acknowledge my friends and teachers at the National Museum of Social Anthropology (Universidade Federal of Rio de Janeiro) for the superb intellectual climate that I enjoyed during my studies there. Among the friends, I thank Luís Rodolfo Vilhena, Celso Castro, Jayme Aranha, Miriam Goldenberg, and Maria Laura Cavalcanti for an always healthy exchange of ideas, along with the members of my doctoral committee — Gilberto Velho, Giralda Seyferth, Lília Schwarcz, Eduardo Viveiros de Castro, and Peter Fry — for their stimulating comments. The National Council for Scientific and Technological Development generously provided me scholarship support, both during my studies in Rio and during my time at Northwestern University.

During that time (1991), my U.S. adviser, Howard S. Becker, enriched my understanding of anthropology and of Brazil. Also at Northwestern, Paul Berliner introduced me to ethnomusicology and to the mbira, an inebriating African percussion instrument. I was pleased to be associated institutionally with Northwestern's Department of Sociology. Many friends helped me feel at home in the United States: Julian, Erik, Matthew, Arto, Doug, Tunji, Norman, Tetê, Glória, Esther, and Dianne.

Other friends, at home, contributed in ways they often little suspected: Luiz, Barrão, Serginho, Sandra, Sílvia, Fausto, Caetano, Carlinhos, Branco Britto, and Lau. I owe a lot to Regina, who read early versions of the manuscript and made suggestions that continue to inspire my research.

For the Brazilian version of the published book, I benefited from the skilled editing of Cristina Zahar and Heloísa Buarque de Holanda. At University of North Carolina Press, I got help and encouragement from David Perry and Elaine Maisner.

Finally, I am grateful to my dissertation adviser, Gilberto Velho, for unfailing intellectual stimulation, for unstinting friendship, for inevitably firm deadlines, for phone calls in the wee hours (like 10 A.M., which for me is a "wee hour"), and above all, for his own pioneering work on the anthropology of complex societies. To contribute, in whatever way, to developing his original ideas would be, for me, the greatest honor of all.

1 The Encounter

I n 1926, "Elegant News," a regular social column in Rio de Janeiro's *Revista da Semana*, first recorded the presence in that
city of a young anthropologist from the northeastern state of
Pernambuco: *Doctor* Gilberto Freyre, as the columnist called
him, making a special point of his title. The soon-to-be-famous
Freyre was visiting the capital of Brazil for the first time at the age
of twenty-six, after completing his university studies in the United
States and after touring several European countries. In various
autobiographical passages of his book *Tempo morto e outros tempos*,
Freyre mentions this odd fact almost proudly. He first set foot in
the principal city of his own country only upon returning from his
travels in the "First World," making plain that his intellectual training had depended not at all on Rio de Janeiro or, in general, on the
Brazilian south, economically and politically the central region of
the country.

In another passage of the same book, Freyre records a singular event that occurred during his stay in Rio. "Sérgio and Prudente," he wrote enthusiastically, "really do know modern English
and French literature. They're tops. I went out for some bohemian fun with them the other night. With Villa-Lobos and Gallet,
too. We went for an evening of guitar music and a drop of *cachaça*
[cane liquor] with three true Brazilians—Pixinguinha, Patrício, and
Donga." The style is a bit telegraphic, so, in order to show the
historical importance of this little remembered "evening of guitar
music," we must clarify the identities of those who participated.
"Sérgio" was the historian Sérgio Buarque de Holanda. "Prudente"
was the Rio district attorney Pedro Dantas Prudente de Moraes
Neto, well-known as a journalist by the pen name "Pedro Dantas."
"Villa-Lobos," of course, was the classical composer Heitor Villa-
Lobos, and "Gallet," Luciano Gallet, was also a classical composer
and pianist. Patrício, Donga, and Pixinguinha were samba players,

the latter two, especially, immortalized by their nicknames in the pantheon of Brazilian popular music.[1]

This encounter thus brought together members of two very distinct social groups: on one hand, intellectuals and practitioners of the "fine" arts, all sons of "good white families," including Prudente de Moraes Neto, the grandson of a Brazilian president, and, on the other hand, musicians of black and mixed race, belonging to the poorest class of Rio society. Here were young Gilberto Freyre and Sérgio Buarque de Holanda, just beginning the research that resulted, a few years later, in their influential books *Casa grande e senzala* (*The Masters and the Slaves*, 1933) and *Raízes do Brasil* (*Roots of Brazil*, 1936), books fundamental to the definition of modern Brazilian identity.[2] And face-to-face with the anthropologist and historian stood Donga, Pixinguinha, and Patrício, whose music would come to stand for what was most Brazilian in Brazil during those same years. The written testimony of the elite participants seems to indicate that they took such a gathering for granted and that both sides felt quite at ease, as well they might in a Brazil supposedly characterized (in Freyre's influential book) by racial mixing and (in Buarque de Holanda's interpretation) by cordial social relations. The only shortcoming, lamented one participant as the evening's activities drew to a close, was "the absence of a few *cabrochinhas* ['wenches' of mixed African and European descent] to make the entertainment complete."[3]

That "night of guitar music" could serve as an allegory, in the carnivalesque meaning of that word, of the "invention of a tradition": the traditional use of samba to represent and define Brazil's cultural and racial "hybridity." Too much should not be made, perhaps, of the naturalness of the episode. Its seeming triviality is obviously constructed. It has the feel of foundational myth. Still, the fact that the gathering was not transformed into myth, nor remembered as something extraordinary by the participants or their biographers, shows that they regarded the event as an everyday occurrence, unworthy of more careful record. This aspect, in fact, is what first attracted me to the event and suggested its significance. If we look behind the scenes, we can observe that many other social circumstances and actors (groups as well as individuals) collaborated to produce the sense of harmony and naturalness surrounding the event in the recollection of the participants.

Let us begin with a rapid panorama of the city where the episode took place: a burgeoning Rio de Janeiro with more than a million inhabitants. In 1926, the presidency of Artur Bernardes—undergirded practically throughout by a decree of martial law—was coming to a close. Bernardes hailed from the powerful state of Minas Gerais and, according to the oligarchical arrangement that governed Brazil during the period 1889–1930, the presidency was due to pass to a representative of the other most powerful state, São Paulo. But signs of the end of the coffee-planting oligarchy's long rule were plainly visible. Uprisings of dissenting junior army officers—"the Lieutenants"—had shaken the cities of Rio and São Paulo, and a similar group even then roamed through the Brazilian backlands, presaging the revolution of 1930. During the presidency of Bernardes, the city of Rio was suffering the uncomfortable sequels of the urban reforms that had been initiated by Mayor Pereira Passos during the first decade of the twentieth century and that had continued through the second, culminating in the massive leveling of a large hill close to the city center, just in time for the erection there of pavilions for an exposition commemorating the centenary of Brazilian independence in 1922. In addition, it was in the decades of the urban reforms that the current north-south division in the sociocultural contours of Rio de Janeiro took definitive shape.

Until the Pereira Passos reforms, downtown Rio de Janeiro had been a heterogeneous jumble of commercial establishments, small manufacturing operations, and government offices, along with residences running the social gamut from the poorest tenements (called *cortiços*, "honeycombs") to the palatial homes of millionaires. The opening of a wide Avenida Central through the densely packed buildings of the old city marked the destruction of the the cortiços and the shift toward a downtown dedicated exclusively to business. The Cariocas, inhabitants of Rio de Janeiro, moved out of the center of town in two directions. The impoverished denizens of the vanishing cortiços took shelter in the new hillside shantytowns called *favelas* scattered throughout the city on ground too steep for other constructions or else moved out along railroad lines to the

North Zone. Meanwhile, the more prosperous former inhabitants of the old downtown settled increasingly in the beachfront neighborhoods of Copacabana and Ipanema in the South Zone, now connected to the city center by a recently excavated tunnel.

The Avenida Central became the city's showcase, the location of such modern attractions as the principal movie houses, and of the cafés so important to Rio's social and intellectual life. Rio was "becoming civilized," said the newspapers, eliding the notions of civilization and modernity. And Rio was declaring itself modern just in time to offer a beachhead for the invasion of artistic modernism. When Gilberto Freyre arrived in Rio in 1926, four years after the first "uprising" of Brazilian modernists in São Paulo's epoch-making Modern Art Week, a local cinema proudly announced the Brazilian debut of yet another Paramount production, titled in Portuguese "The Jazz Epidemic": "Don't be afraid. It is futurism. You may find it unhinged. But we guarantee you'll like it and discover it has a very special flavor all its own." The newspaper ad went on to say proudly that the movie would be preceded by a live presentation featuring the actress Iracema de Alencar, star of the Casino Theater, exploring "the absurd, the illogical, and the irreverent."[4] Carioca popular culture had not tarried long in carnivalizing the absurdist teachings of São Paulo's artistic vanguard.

Observing these transformations, the non-Carioca Gilberto Freyre waxed oddly nostalgic for a Rio that he never knew and directed biting criticisms at the new buildings and boulevards and at the leveling of the hills. "In the presence of horrors like the Elixir building, one gets the impression of jokes played by the architects on the nouveaux riches that ordered up these novelties," Freyre wrote in his diary, and went on: "The new Chamber of Deputies is downright ridiculous. That Roman-style statue of Deodoro would make a cat smile."[5] Freyre inveighed against broad boulevards like the new Avenida Central and found virtue in narrow streets like the Rua do Ouvidor, formerly Rio's most prestigious, because these were shady and therefore more appropriate to the tropical heat. He even approved of the ramshackle neighborhood on Favela hill (which subsequently gave its name to hillside slums throughout Brazil) as a piece of old Rio.[6]

But let us get back to the matter of Freyre's "bohemian fun" in the irremediably new Rio of the 1920s and, more particularly, the matter of the nocturnal diversions involving both elite males and "true Brazilians" like the samba players Donga, Pixinguinha, and Patrício. To bring together people representing such different aspects of Rio de Janeiro, the young Brazilian intellectuals had called upon an extensive network of personal relationships.

Sérgio Buarque de Holanda and Prudente de Moraes Neto, who had so impressed Freyre with their knowledge of modern English and French literature, were editors of the literary magazine Estética. Buarque de Holanda was from São Paulo, epicenter of Brazilian artistic modernism, and he had introduced Prudente de Moraes Neto, a Carioca, to modern art well before Modern Art Week in 1922. The two had met at law school in Rio. Moraes Neto must have been receptive to the attractions of modern art. Another former classmate, who had known Prudente at Pedro II Secondary School (where sons of the Brazilian elite had congregated for generations), said this president's grandson had a "taste for the strange."[7] A shared taste for European literary modernism, at any rate, brought together the two young editors of Estética and the equally young and as yet unknown—but already extremely presumptuous—anthropologist from Pernambuco, Gilberto Freyre.

Moraes Neto and Buarque de Holanda differ on how they first got wind of Freyre. Moraes Neto recalled a letter from Luís da Câmara Cascudo (later distinguished as a folklorist) containing a clipping of an article written by Freyre about James Joyce for a Pernambucan newspaper.[8] Buarque de Holanda remembered receiving the clipping in a letter from the future regionalist novelist of the northeast José Lins do Rego some time after announcing that Estética would publish criticism of James Joyce: "The name of the [clipping's] author was as unknown to me, to any of us, as the name of the letter writer. I don't have the article anymore, but I clearly remember a crack about critics who, 'in the shade of Carioca banana trees' have the audacity to announce an up-coming article on so difficult a writer as Joyce."[9] Freyre's exact words appeared in the Diário de Pernambuco on 11 November 1926: "Even under the banana trees of Rio people are saying the easily pronounced English name Joyce. The English of his works will be more difficult to decipher."[10] Freyre's ironic words ended up seducing these modernists-under-banana-trees. Buarque de Holanda says that he liked the article so much that he decided to republish it in Estética and shelve the criticism that he had been planning to write himself. As things turned out, though, the magazine folded first.

Thus began—under the sign of James Joyce—this Brazilian interregional modernist alliance. The Cariocas were surprised to see such an up-to-date study appear in the "provincial" press of the northeast, and they immediately struck up a correspondence with its author. Their friendship was not the result of a mutual interest in Brazilian popular culture and much less in the regionalist vein of that popular culture, but that interest soon became a factor. Among the curiosities that brought the northeasterner to Rio de Janeiro in 1926 was "a desire for direct contact with the composers and performers of Carioca popular music, especially the black ones."[11] At the time, black samba players from Rio de Janeiro were touring the country with great success. Freyre was away in New York when the Carioca group Oito Batutas performed in Pernambuco in 1921, but he surely heard the signal influence that performance had on the musicians of his home state.

For starters, Sérgio Buarque de Holanda and Prudente de Moraes Neto took Freyre to the show called "Tudo Preto" ("All Black"), presented by the Black Revue Company, Brazil's first theater group with exclusively black performers and staff—including the maestro Pixinguinha, and the director, whose artistic name was De Chocolat. Only the impresario was white. "All Black" caused a furor in Rio during that year's theatrical season. One newspaper called the show "the biggest theatrical news of the moment," a show producing "magnificent spiritual pleasure" in the audience.[12] Another paper used the adjective estrondoso—"smashing"—and remarked on the throng that attended its opening night. None of the journalists or critics was shocked by the exclusive presence of black people on stage, as if that were not really extraordinary, and all applauded the initiative. But the publicity of the Revue could not contain its pride in "a victory for the black race in light theater." It was a victory, too, for the performer called "Miss Mons" (a "French eccentric," announced *Correio da manhã*, tongue in cheek), who executed "an authentic African *batuque*," the drumming and dancing of Brazilian slaves.

Gilberto Freyre esteemed the batuque of Miss Mollis, but the music of Pixinguinha excited him most, and he wanted to meet the famous sambista, as samba players and dancers are known, in a more casual setting, without the black tie and tuxedo that Pixinguinha wore on stage in "All Black." Freyre's friends drew on a tangle of personal connections to fulfill his wish. Fortunately, Prudente knew a member of Pixinguinha's band, Donga. Prudente and Donga had been introduced by Blaise Cendrars (an interesting foreign intervention in the elite "discovery" of Carioca popular culture), during that French vanguardist poet's 1924 stay in Rio. Two years later, in an effort to organize an informal musical gathering for his Pernambucan friend, Prudente got back in touch with Donga. The black sambista was playing backup for a band called Carlito Jazz, part of a "gay and naughty" French revue company then offering spectacles entitled "C'est Paris," "Au revoir," and "Revue de la revue." The gathering was to take place in a café on Catete Street, across from the law school in a heterogeneous neighborhood just outside the city center. That night, the café closed its doors for the privacy of its special guests. In addition to Donga, Pixinguinha, and Patrício, two other outstanding sambistas were in attendance: Sebastião Cirino, whose song "Christ Was Born in Bahia" was the great hit of the day,[13] and, apparently, Nelson Alves, another of the Oito Batutas.

Perhaps by oversight, Prudente's account of the evening does not mention the presence of Heitor Villa-Lobos, about which Freyre's diary is very clear. On the other hand, it could be Freyre's lapse, expressing his desire to identify the musical nationalism of Villa-Lobos with Rio's Afro-Brazilian bohemia. Villa-Lobos was, in fact, a carousing night owl well liked among the city's sambistas. Freyre's association of Villa-Lobos with the Carioca mystique is exemplified in another reminiscence written years later:

My friend Assis Chateaubriand initiated me into various Carioca-style Brazilianisms, and Estácio Coimbra, into others.

Finally, with Prudente de Moraes Neto, Sérgio Buarque de Holanda, and Jaime Ovalle I became initiated into another sort of Brazilianism, the Afro-Carioca and nocturnal Rio, so to speak. The Rio of Pixinguinha and Patrício. The still almost colonial Rio of guitars, serenades, and colored wenches [mulatas] whose Brazilian authenticity lent them a grace, shared by the white "missies" [iaiás] of Botafogo or the ladies [sinhás] of Santa Teresa [two traditionally fashionable Rio neighborhoods], a grace I never saw in the mulatas or the iaiás of the North. It was the Carioca grace. It was the Rio of Villa-Lobos.[14]

The northeastern regionalist Gilberto Freyre was being seduced by Carioca popular culture. And Freyre was not the only one: from the 1930s on, all Brazil began (or was obliged) to recognize in the samba of Rio de Janeiro an emblem of its national identity.

Another reference to the 1926 gathering in the Catete Street café appears in an article published by Freyre in a Pernambucan newspaper later that year, an article suggestively entitled "On the Valorization of Things Black." Freyre's tone differs from that of the newspaper's ordinary journalistic articles. The polemical northeasterner missed no opportunity to advance his ideas—later systematically developed in books like *The Masters and the Slaves*—on the importance of Brazil's African heritage. His style is almost always militant, ready to raise hackles among his readers if need be. Here are his words:

> Yesterday, along with some friends—Prudente and Sérgio—I spent an evening-that-almost-reached-morning listening to Pixinguinha, a mulato, playing some of his carnival music accompanied by Donga, another mulato, on the guitar and by a (really black) black fellow, Patrício, singing. A wonderful, Carioca-style Brazilian night.
>
> As we listened, the three of us could feel the great Brazil that is growing half-hidden by the phony and ridiculous official Brazil where mulatos emulate Greeks . . . and *caboclos* [country people of Portuguese and indigenous ancestry] try to appear Europeans and North Americans; everyone looking stupidly at

things Brazilian . . . through the pince-nez of a Frenchified doctor of laws.[15]

Freyre's article returns to the theory of two antagonistic "Brazils," popularized principally by Euclides da Cunha in *Os sertões* (translated into English as *Rebellion in the Backlands*) a generation earlier, with a stronger emphasis on the need to "valorize" the Brazil that defied European models. Gilberto Freyre declared official Brazil a "phony and ridiculous" Europhile version that "hid" the real Brazil, personified for him by black musicians.

The article begins by affirming that "in Rio there is a movement to assert the value of things black." The two causes given to explain this movement of affirmation are very interesting. One is the "influence of Blaise Cendrars, who now comes to Rio every year for carnival." The influence of Cendrars (and the way that Brazilian intellectuals represented his influence) will be examined in a later chapter. The second cause adduced by Freyre to account for the "valorization" of things black was a more abstract "tendency toward sincerity," as pointed out by Prudente de Moraes in an article in *Estética*. According to Prudente, Brazilians were becoming "sincere enough to recognize that they are steeped in black influences."[16] Popular music would be a fundamental element in the valorization of black culture. Freyre adopted the style of a manifesto to proclaim that "black song forms, black dances, mixed with traces of *fado* [a distinctively Portuguese musical tradition] . . . are perhaps the best thing Brazil has to offer."[17] The discovery of samba was under way.

2 The Mystery

There is a great mystery in the history of samba. I do not refer to any of the problems that most researchers of Brazilian popular music so enjoy debating: the etymology of the word *samba*, the precise birthplace of the music, the names of the first sambistas, or the definitive list of players involved in the collective composition of "Pelo telefone" ("On the Telephone"), normally held to be "the first samba." Rather, I am thinking of samba's transformation into a "national rhythm," when it was suddenly "discovered" by the nation as a whole and adopted as a defining element of *brasilidade* or Brazilian identity.

Until now, practically all attempts to write a history of samba contain the same gap—a complete discontinuity separating two moments in the narrative. At issue is the relationship between Carioca sambistas, on one hand, and the rest of Brazilian society (especially the elite), on the other. The first moment is the repression of samba, a time when the music was sequestered in the favelas of Rio, limited to the "popular classes." In the second moment, the sambistas triumph in carnival and on the radio, becoming symbols of Brazil as a whole, establishing relationships with all sectors of Brazilian society, constituting a new image of the country intended for both internal and international consumption. Samba's unexplained leap from infamous outcast to (virtually official) national emblem, a transformation conventionally mentioned only in passing, is the great mystery of its history. This book will construct its argument around this mystery, represented here (problematically of course, as in all representations) by the encounter between Freyre, Pixinguinha, and their respective friends.

A good conventional summary of how samba was transformed into a national music appears in the postscript of Antônio Cândido's notable article on Brazilian culture and the revolution of 1930:

In popular music there occurred a process . . . of "generalization" and "normalization" this time flowing from poorer social groups to the middle and upper classes. In the 1930s and 1940s, for example, samba and *marcha* [a related, somewhat slower musical form], practically confined to the favelas and poor peripheral neighborhoods in previous years, won over the whole country, becoming the daily bread of cultural consumption for all social classes. During the 1920s, a master sambista like Sinhô performed in restricted settings, but after 1930 sambistas like Noel Rosa, Ismael Silva, Almirante, Lamartine Babo, João da Bahiana, Nássara, João de Barro, and many others gained national recognition. They prepared the way for the overpowering triumph of popular music in the 1960s, when it even became the partner of highbrow poetry in a breaking down of barriers that constitutes one of the most important facts of our contemporary culture. This interpenetration began with the interest in "things Brazilian" that followed the revolution of 1930.[1]

Chroniclers of samba have generally agreed. A good example can be found in the classic collection of articles by Jota Efegê: "In those vanished times of 1920 until almost 1930, samba was considered illegitimate. It was looked on as the stuff of lowlife rascals, the carol of vagabonds. And the police, in their chief function of watching over the maintenance of public order, persecuted [samba] without rest."[2] The same chronicler also presents the other side of the coin, popular resistance: "The heroic epoch was like that, its people valiant, not letting themselves be intimidated, battered but unrelenting," ignoring "the scorn of the bourgeoisie." And "samba won the day in spite of everything. It formed its parading groups and astonished both countrymen and foreigners."[3] As always, the mysterious transition from police persecution to unanimous celebration is announced but not explained.

Anthropologists, too, generally accept the basic outlines of this story wherein samba was restricted to the favelas until abruptly triumphing in the musical taste of a social elite previously quite distant from Afro-Brazilian popular culture. Peter Fry affirms that "originally, when samba was produced and consumed by the people of the favelas, it was severely repressed by the police and forced to conceal itself in *candomblé* [Afro-Brazilian religion], which was then considered slightly more acceptable. Meanwhile, with the passage of time, the growing importance of carnival provoked a transformation from repression to open support." [4] A few years later, Fry's words were echoed by Ruben Oliven: "Samba, another legitimate symbol of Brazilian culture, was at first produced and consumed in the favelas of Rio de Janeiro and violently repressed by the police. It was with the growing importance of carnival that samba began to be consumed by the rest of the Brazilian population, becoming transformed into the Brazilian music *par excellence*." [5]

The mystery of samba's abrupt "discovery" is linked to other pivotal mysteries in the debate over the definition of Brazilian national identity. Antônio Cândido refers to the interest in "things Brazilian" that arose among the revolutionaries of 1930. What were these "things Brazilian"? Who decided what things were definitively Brazilian and thus worthy of that interest? How did an elite that had supposedly paid scant attention to Brazilian popular culture acquire an appreciation for things such as samba or *feijoada* (a black bean meal formerly scorned by the well-to-do), which little by little became the "national dish," proudly served to foreign visitors? How, above all, did racial mixture, principally between whites and blacks, gain prominence among official national values?

Just as samba is a central mystery of Brazilian popular music, race mixing is a central mystery of Brazilian social thought. During the late nineteenth century and into the twentieth, scientific theories of racial degeneration had stigmatized race mixing as a principal cause of Brazil's problems. How could the 1933 publication of Gilberto Freyre's acclaimed challenge to those theories in *The Masters and the Slaves* work such a sudden transformation—making race mixing the guarantor of Brazil's special cultural identity, the mark of our unique "tropicalist civilization"—almost overnight? Freyre's success on the intellectual scene and the simultaneous broadening of interest in samba, conceived as a musical blending of white and black culture, constituted parallel manifestations of the new interest in "things Brazilian." An understanding of both is necessary if we are fully to understand either. And why, above all, did these mysterious transformations occur? As we will see, Freyre described *The Masters and the Slaves* as the result of a sudden spiritual illumination, leading to "a kind of psychoanalytic cure" for the whole country, but this and similar explanations⁶ only underline the mysterious abruptness and discontinuity implied in the narratives of "discovery," in which the true Brazil, so long hidden by the false Brazil, is suddenly uncovered and its true value recognized.

Further complexities emerge when the mystery of samba is placed in an international context. Here we might take up a question posed by Peter Fry. "Why is it that in Brazil the producers of national symbols and mass culture selected cultural items originally generated by dominated groups? And why did this not occur in the United States and in other capitalist societies?"⁷ Although problematically oversimplifying both the Brazilian and the U.S. case, the question correctly highlights the importance of class hierarchy in Brazil. Fry answered his own question by hypothesizing that "the conversion of ethnic symbols into national symbols masks a situation of racial domination and makes it especially difficult to uncover."⁸ Roberto da Matta deconstructs the race-mixing myth through reference, once again, to the "powerfully hierarchical" nature of Brazilian notions of society. Da Matta suggests that there is less need to maintain segregation among the various racial groups in Brazil because the internalization of these hierarchies assures the superiority of whites as the dominant group. Hence the Brazilian preoccupation—here da Matta and Fry converge—with forms of intermediation and syncretism. Synthesis impedes open conflict by diverting "a crude, naked perception of the mechanisms of social and political exploitation."⁹

Roberto da Matta's arguments may account for the relative absence of racial segregation in Brazil, but they do not totally elucidate the powerful sociocultural investment that leads us to identify "things Brazilian" with racial and cultural mixing, principally between blacks and whites. Nor do they explain what led Freyre and company to meet with Pixinguinha and company on Catete Street in 1926, a moment so important for the flowering of an "authentic" and previously "hidden" Brazil. To accept samba as an element of authentic Brazilian culture is one thing, and to raise it up as the very symbol of Brazilian cultural uniqueness is quite another. Even Thomas Skidmore, in an article that presents abundant quantitative proof of strong racism in Brazil (and thus denies the existence of great differences in racial attitudes between it and the United States), recognizes "the persistent negrophobia of U.S. whites" to be "a trait relatively absent in Brazilian history." [10] In addition, Skidmore notes that "the continuing reality of miscegenation in English America was transformed by white males into a psychological threat." [11] Meanwhile, a similar reality became a theme of national pride for Brazilian authors like Gilberto Freyre.

The foregoing hypotheses and comparisons will now be explored through a detailed analysis of the process by which samba became a Brazilian national symbol. As foreshadowed by the description of the Catete Street encounter, special attention will be directed to the relationship of intellectuals to popular culture, especially popular music. Rather than an anthropology of samba for its own sake, this is a study of the role of popular culture in the construction of national identity. It takes music as a field of heightened importance in the struggle to define Brazilian culture and chooses samba—among many other possible choices—as a primary vehicle to examine various aspects of the process. Brazilian rock music might have constituted the object of a similar set of reflections, but samba, as "the daily bread of our cultural consumption" and "Brazilian music *par excellence*" occupies a more central place in the debate over Brazilian identity.

This centrality has been amply recognized. We have seen how Antônio Cândido characterized the triumph of 1960s popular music as "one of the most important facts of our contemporary culture." Referring to an earlier stage of the same phenomenon in 1939, the modernist writer Mário de Andrade celebrated the rise of Brazilian popular music as "the most powerful creation and most beautiful characterization of our race." [12] Gilberto Freyre called music "the most Brazilian of arts" and the privileged manifestation of "the pre-national and national spirit of the Luso-American people, whether aristocratic, bourgeois, plebeian, or rustic." [13] These scholars and others have perceived music, more than other sorts of artistic expression, as having the potential to break down

barriers of race and class and serve as a unifying element, a chan-
nel of communication, among diverse groups in Brazilian society.
The veracity of that belief matters less, for our purposes here,
than does its salience for many of the intellectuals who have been
involved, over the years, in the discussion surrounding various aspects of our national identity.

Rather than to unravel the mystery of samba altogether, my object is more precisely to displace it in time. I intend to show that
samba's transformation into a national music was less a sudden
leap from repression to acclamation in less than a decade and
much more the culmination of a gradual process. Thus, the encounter described in this chapter is only one example of a tradition
of encounters among various social groups that collectively, and
over centuries, invented Brazilian identity and popular culture. My
intention is not to deny the repression of elements of popular culture. Instead, I will show how repression coexisted with other types
of social interaction occasionally contrary to repression. I will try
to map the relations between Rio's first sambistas and other social
groups to show how they paved the way for the great majority of
the Brazilian population to embrace samba, or at least to accept it
as the quasi-official national music of Brazil. I will also attempt to
trace related debates that arose among members of the Brazilian
elite over national unity and race mixing, for example, and especially concerning elite attitudes toward "the people." These debates led some factions of the elite (never a monolithic group, any
more than were "the people") to seek out and cultivate relationships with sambistas.

Rather than the discovery of true cultural roots formerly ob-
scured by repression, the transformation of samba into a national
music will be presented here as a process whereby the notion of
samba's authenticity was itself invented and cultivated. The "discovery" of samba by the young Brazilian intellectuals of the 1920s
provides examples of "the invention of tradition" or "the fabrication of authenticity," in the formulations advanced by Eric
Hobsbawm and Richard Peterson, respectively.[14] I subscribe to the
words of Peterson, in his description of the invention of U.S. country music: "Authenticity is not a trait inherent in an object or an

event that one declares 'authentic'; it is a matter of social construction, a convention that partially deforms the past."[15] I agree with Néstor García Canclini that popular culture "is constructed through complex, hybrid processes, using elements from diverse classes and nations as signs of identification."[16] In this perspective, one can affirm, without recklessness, that the poor black inhabitants of Rio de Janeiro favelas did not create samba in isolation from the rest of Brazilian society, that people of other classes, other races, even other nationalities participated in the process, if only as active spectators who encouraged musical performances. Hence, this study will emphasize the "external relations," so to speak, of the sambistas' world.

The following chapters will explore various problems raised by our description of the 1926 encounter in the Catete Street café, the phenomena that made the meeting possible, and their consequences for the invention of Brazilian popular culture. The meeting constitutes an excellent point of departure for our meditations on the invention of Brazil's "national-popular" traditions because it brought together the principal elements requiring analysis: the relations between elites and the "popular" classes; the valorization of "the popular"; the creation of a new national identity; theories of racial and cultural mixing; the "discovery" of Brazil by modernist intellectuals; the tension between "regionalism" and Rio-centered "unity"; the various currents of nationalist discourse; and samba as "the best Brazil has to offer." Let us begin with the Brazilian elite's historical relationship to popular music.

3 Popular Music and the Brazilian Elite

he encounter described in the preceding chapter was hardly an extraordinary event in the history of Brazilian popular music. It fit into a long tradition of social relations bringing together various manifestations of Afro-Brazilian musical culture with elite intellectuals, writers, politicians, landowners, and aristocrats.

This is an old story. Its beginnings, or at least the first clear pieces of evidence, go back to the *modinha* and the *lundu*, two musical forms popularized in the late eighteenth century, when Brazil was still a Portuguese colony. In a book published in 1805, the traveler Thomas Lindley provides the following narration of festive gatherings in the northeastern Brazilian city of Salvador, Bahia, at the turn of the nineteenth century: "A few of the superior classes give elegant entertainments, have family concerts, balls, and card parties. During and after [their banquets] they drink unusual quantities of wine; and when elevated to an extraordinary pitch, the guitar or violin is introduced and singing commences. But the song soon gives way to the enticing *Negro dance* . . . which is a mixture of the dances of Africa and the fandangos of Spain and Portugal."[1] This description reveals a Bahian elite impatient with the constraints of elegant European-style deportment. A few glasses of wine put them in the mood for "black" music and dancing—"black," or better, already racially and culturally mixed. Lindley points out the choreographical fusion between African and Iberian dances. That fusion, beginning so long ago, is likely to foil any attempt to establish what is really African or European in Brazilian popular dancing today.

The Bahian elite at least tried to render homage to European etiquette early in the evening, which does not seem to have been the case everywhere in Brazil. Another foreign traveler, L. F. de Tollenare, complained that in the salons of Pernambuco during the same period, "people knew how to dance only lundu."[2] This tendency might be explained, as Gilberto Freyre proposes, by the isolation of white elites in the colonial period.[3] But a look at the larger context suggests a different explanation. A brief history of the modinha, the more lyrical cousin of the lundu, shows that even the Portuguese aristocracy resident in Lisbon was allowing itself to be seduced by imported products of Afro-Brazilian cultural fusion. The rules of European etiquette may not have been so rigid, after all.

The initial popularizer of the modinha, and the man who crystallized it as a musical form, was Domingos Caldas Barbosa, a priest of mixed black and white ancestry from Rio de Janeiro and Brazil's "first historically recognized composer," according to historians of Brazilian popular music. José Ramos Tinhorão, the most important of those historians, describes the modinha as the Brazilian style of playing Portuguese lyric songs called *modas*, a style invented principally by people of the popular class and of mixed race. Brazilian modinhas turned most frequently—and in a more frankly libidinous manner than did their Portuguese models—on amorous themes, accompanied principally by stringed instruments such as the guitar or the mandolin.[4] Caldas Barbosa's "condition" as the son of an Angolan mother and a white father did not keep him from becoming a success when, in 1775, he performed in the most aristocratic salons of Lisbon—though not without some protest. The voices raised against the modinha, somewhat surprisingly, were those of Portuguese poets Bocage, Filinto Elíseo, and Antônio Ribeiro dos Santos, the last of whom went so far as to consider the presence of the Brazilian musician "an indicator of the dissolution of the Portuguese court."[5]

Interestingly, those whom one would think most directly threatened by Caldas Barbosa's success in propagating his risqué colonial modinhas did not react the same way. Soon erudite Portuguese composers began to produce their own modinhas. Since Portuguese composers generally studied their craft in Italy, the result was the "Italianization" of the modinha, which assimilated influences common to the Italian operettas by Bellini and Donizetti then playing to full houses in Lisbon. Clothed in its new Italianate attire, the modinha then returned to Brazil in 1808, along with the Portuguese royal family (which was exiting Lisbon to flee Napoleon and set up its court in Rio de Janeiro). In Rio and in Salvador, the new version of the modinha influenced local forms and itself underwent a process that Tinhorão calls "re-popularization and re-nationalization."[6] Thus, the back-and-forth movement of international musical influences far antedates the advent of the phonograph or the electronic mass media. In fact, the modinha made several successive return voyages to Europe in the nineteenth century. Sigismund Neukomm, one of Hayden's favorite students, lived five years in Rio and later published arrangements of modinhas in Paris, showing the continued cultural permeability not only of international frontiers but also of those between classical and popular music. Carlos Gomes, the outstanding Brazilian operatic and orchestral composer of the nineteenth century, signed his name to various modinhas.[7]

After the proclamation of Brazil's independence by Emperor Pedro I in 1822, the modinha became an integral part of life at the Brazilian imperial court, or at least, of life in certain corners of that court. For example, the emperor's mistress, the Marquesa de Santos, "when among intimate friends at the parties she gave in São Cristóvão, sang melancholy modinhas and lundus, accompanying herself on the gently plucked strings of the plaintive [guitar]."[8] According to her biographer, Carlos Maul, the distinguished men who gathered around the Marquesa—powerful deputies, senators, and ministers—also cultivated the Brazilian popular music of the day. Januário da Cunha Barbosa, canon of the Imperial Chapel and director of both Rio's public library and the national press, was said to "put aside politics to play the guitar and sing modinhas" at such gatherings.[9]

During the middle years of the nineteenth century, the renovation—or "re-nationalization"—of the modinha occurred with the participation of several different segments of Brazilian society. Quoting Freyre: "The modinha . . . was a musical agent of Brazilian unification sung, as it was during the reign of the second emperor, by some to the sound of pianos inside bourgeois and noble houses, by others to the sound of guitars in the night air at the door of even humble shacks."[10] But the phenomenon that most contributed to the renewal of the modinha at midcentury was the interaction of popular-class musicians with young intellectuals and romantic writers. Their principal meeting place was at the press of "mulatto editor and poet Francisco de Paula Brito,"[11] in Rio's Constitution Square, which attracted such leading literary lights as Joaquim Maria Machado de Assis and José de Alencar, chief novelists of the nineteenth century, and Antônio Gonçalves Dias, the century's most celebrated poet, as well as Laurindo Rabelo, a musician and poet of Gypsy ancestry, and "instrumentalists of the popular classes."[12] As we have seen, such encounters between elite intellectuals and poor musicians would be repeated years later in the history of the samba.

According to Eunice Ribeiro Gondim, biographer of Paula Brito, "the whole feverish, Romantic generation of 1839–1861" frequented these gatherings.[13] Paula Brito's shop was the scene of meetings by the group of friends (and enemies) later called the Petalogical Society (from the word peta, meaning fabrication). Machado de Assis, who got his start working for Paula Brito in the 1850s, described the Society as the place

> where everybody went—politicians, poets, playwrights, artists, travelers, or simply friends, amateurs, the merely curious— where everything was talked about, from the resignation of a government minister to the pirouettes of currently modish dancers, where everything was argued over, from Tamberlick's heartache to the speeches of the Marquis of Paraná, a true neutral ground where the literary beginner met with the imperial councillor, where Italian singers conversed with ex-ministers.[14]

Mello de Moraes Filho has collected additional recollections about the print shop of Paula Brito. There, apparently, the maestro Francisco Manuel, "to take a break from his lengthy, sacred compositions," wrote lundus.[15] This testimony makes clear that Paula Brito was an intercultural mediator and that his print shop was truly a "neutral" territory, enabling encounters between members of contrasting social groups.

The existence of such mediators, and of social spaces where

such mediations could take place, is a notion fundamental to un-
raveling the mystery of samba. Brazilian culture is a heterogeneous
culture, one in which we can discern "the coexistence, harmonious or not, of a plurality of traditions whose bases may be occu-
pational, ethnic, [or] religious," to mention only a few possibilities.[16] Heterogeneity is, indeed, a chief characteristic of complex
societies — "the never-finished product of interactions and negotiations among groups, even individuals, whose interests are, in
principle, potentially divergent."[17] This situation makes possible
the constitution of what Gilberto Velho has called "singular individuality" or "radical individualization": "The more exposed to di-
versified experiences, the more an actor realizes the possibility of
contrasting worldviews. The less closed his network of daily relations, the more marked is his potential perception of singular individuality."[18] These "radical" individuals can facilitate — intensify,
accelerate, even institutionalize — relations among the various cultural "worlds" that make up heterogeneous, complex societies.[19]

One of the principal cultural mediators among those who gathered at the printing office of Francisco de Paula Brito was Laurindo
Rabelo, a musician and also an army doctor. A few details about
Rabelo's life will provide examples of the possibilities of this kind
of cultural mediation during the middle years of the nineteenth
century. Rabelo's family had suffered the consequences of a royal
order of 1718, which decreed the deportation of gypsies from Portugal to the Brazilian colony. Laurindo was born in Rio de Janeiro,
and he grew up poor in the 1820s and 1830s, according to Mello
de Moraes Filho, feeling early "the social prejudice . . . that ostra-
cized the tawny troubador as a person of mixed-blood."[20] Despite
his "blonde" hair, Laurindo was not considered to be white. If race
prejudice kept him from consummating "the love of his youth," it
did not constitute a barrier to his eventually gaining artistic (and
intellectual) celebrity among the imperial elite. After making an
initial attempt to become a military officer and after considering
the priesthood, Rabelo entered Rio's medical school, one of only
two in Brazil. But he encountered financial difficulties and found a
powerful patron, an imperial councillor who sponsored his trans-
fer to the Brazilian empire's other medical school, in Salvador,

Bahia. Upon graduation, he returned to Rio and became a military doctor, but he was soon sent away to the southern part of the country because of a conflict with his superior officer. Never did his medical studies replace music, nor his military duties banish poetry from his life. To the contrary, the fame of his poetry spread throughout Brazil and elite admirers called him "our Bocage"—a highly flattering comparison to the great eighteenth-century Portuguese poet. Mello de Moraes Filho says that the "gypsy troubador" was in high demand for "*sarάos de família*"—musical soirees given in the homes of Rio's elite families. Here is a description of one such event: "In general, after it was late at night, when the music was getting strident and the floor boiled with whirling dancers, a certain number of admirers would cluster in a corner of the dining room around Laurindo, who, minstrel and bard, sang sentimental modinhas and rowdy lundus to the music of a guitar." [21]

Another musician of the period who mediated among social groups was Alexandre Trovador, described by Mello de Moraes Filho as a "clever, sagacious, and able . . . little nigger [creoulinho]." [22] Alexandre learned to be a hairdresser at the salon run by Frederico Reis, located near Paula Brito's print shop on Constitution Square. The Reis shop and the ladies it attracted illustrate the cultural promiscuity, so to speak, of life in Constitution Square. Reis counted in his clientele some of the empire's most distinguished noble families. Alexandre's reputation as a hairdresser became formidable, and he began to receive requests from countesses and baronesses to do hair at luxurious residences, and also from French actresses on tour in Rio. He even visited the imperial palace to attend Princess Isabel and the empress. But Alexandre's real triumph lay not in fancy coiffure, but in his voice, described as a mixture of soprano and contralto, which utterly captivated Rio. Alexandre Trovador sang Italian opera arias and Brazilian modinhas and accompanied both himself on the guitar, which he apparently played quite well. Moraes Filho says that "the phenomenal Trovador made an epoch," though this did not keep him from dying in poverty or being buried in a common grave. [23]

Among other important musicians active in Rio de Janeiro during the second half of the nineteenth century, we could mention several other black men: João Rolas, Anacleto de Medeiros, Eduardo das Neves, and those known simply as Tinoco and Sinhô das Crioulas—the latter so named because of his romantic dedication to very dark-skinned women.[24] However fleeting these performers' fame, race did not seem an impediment to their artistic recognition in the eyes of the Carioca elite.

More important than any of these mid-nineteenth-century musicians (and one of our best sources of information on them, too) was Catulo da Paixão Cearense. Catulo was born in 1863 and lived well into the twentieth century. His period of activity as a cultural mediator extended through the belle epoque during which occurred what a number of scholars have depicted as a total separation of elite from popular culture in Rio de Janeiro. Jeffrey Needell, for example, has written that during this "tropical belle epoque" the dominant desire among elite reformers was "to put an end to that old Brazil, that 'African' Brazil that threatened their claims to Civilization."[25] Mônica Velloso expresses the same opinion: "The apotheosis of the Parisian model of civilization was the concomitant of a loss of prestige for our own traditions. . . . More than ever, popular culture was viewed negatively to the degree that it did not fit the values of modernity." Velloso goes on to say that "in stylish salons, in cafés, and at literary lectures any reference to things native became the height of poor taste."[26] The desire to "re-Europeanize" Brazil (in Freyre's term) may have been dominant among the elite, but if so, it was dominant ma non troppo. Even Rio's belle epoque had countercurrents, that is, practices, some surviving from an earlier time, some new, that embodied a completely different sort of relationship between elite and popular culture.[27]

The life of Catulo da Paixão Cearense illustrates some of these countercurrents. He grew up in the interior of Ceará (hence the name by which he became known) in northern Brazil but came to Rio at the age of seventeen with his father, a goldsmith and a reader of the classics. Father and son took up residence in the fashionable neighborhood of Botafogo, but their financial situation was precarious, and when the father died in 1885, Catulo had to work in the port as stevedore. Even while employed at this rough job, Catulo also sang at "saráos de família" given in the homes of the well-to-do. It was at one such that he met Gaspar Silveira Martins, a member of the imperial council, who shortly thereafter invited Catulo to move into his house and tutor his children in Portuguese. Catulo's singing began to win him numerous admirers in the lofty social circles where he now moved, for example, at the "musico-literary" soirees of Senator Hermenegildo de Morais. He also sang at the house of Mello de Moraes Filho, who (long before writing his famous volumes of folklore, several times cited here) was also involved in promoting a late-nineteenth-century revival of various sorts of folk pageants.[28] Other elite Cariocas were sponsoring similar activities as the turn of the century approached. One was Alberto Brandão, whose regular guests included Sílvio Romero (the period's most important literary critic and a folklorist himself) and Raul Villa-Lobos (always accompanied by his young son, Heitor). During memorable evenings of music at the Brandão residence, the various folk genres of northeastern Brazil were amply represented.[29] In the middle of its belle epoque, Rio de Janeiro was experiencing a vogue for folk music from distant regions of Brazil. José Ramos Tinhorão has described "a taste for the national exotic cultivated in the salons of the first decade of the twentieth century as folklore became stylish,"[30] and indeed, the first important studies of Brazilian folklore were then being published.

Catulo da Paixão Cearense was a very well connected performer. A friend of politicians, writers, and millionaires, he also maintained contact with musicians less famous than himself, including many of the future inventors of samba, and he frequented the house of the famous Bahiana woman Aunt Ciata, one of the fabled cradles of Rio's samba culture. As a legitimate northeasterner, Catulo eventually took advantage of this new interest in the folk culture of the northeastern backlands. But his initial repertory was composed primarily of modinhas, of which he became an acknowledged master—most especially because of a celebrated 1906 performance at a soiree given by Mello de Moraes Filho. One witness to Catulo's moment of glory in the salons of Rio described the applause as "a true explosion of delirium, so loud, so resonant, so spontaneous that a formidable typhoon seemed to shake the room."[31] Catulo supposedly brought tears to the eyes of Rui Barbosa, the acclaimed statesman and author, when he sang at Barbosa's house in Bota-fogo. In 1908, he took his guitar to the National Institute of Music, that bastion of high culture, and sang modinhas there. And in 1914, Catulo sang at the presidential palace. The invitation to do so came from Nair de Teffé, wife of the president, who later discussed the matter in an interview with Catulo's biographer: "In the Brazil of those days . . . everybody sang in foreign languages, mainly in French, Italian, and German. I only sang in those languages my-self."[32] She went on to credit Catulo with the idea of highlighting Brazilian genres and the idea of her performing them herself.

Nair de Teffé's boldness in singing popular song forms at the presidential palace was a bit less pioneering than she implies. As we have seen, Brazilian popular music had graced some of the capi-tal's most prestigious salons for years. Still, Rui Barbosa, the very same who reportedly became teary-eyed listening to Catulo da Pai-xão Cearense, was not above publicly lambasting his political ene-mies for allowing the performance of certain popular airs in the presidential palace, "with honors as if for the music of Wagner."[33] (Barbosa's righteous indignation appears a matter of political ex-pediency.) The fact is that the rhythms of popular music had en-tered the precincts of power long before 1914. Twenty years earlier, one of Rio's early carnival street parading groups had performed for President Floriano Peixoto in the presidential palace. This group was called O Rei de Ouro (loosely, King of Diamonds—the play-ing cards of the period had a suit of ouros, gold coins, instead of diamonds), and it had been formed to introduce to Rio the Afro-Brazilian carnival activities of Bahia. The creator of O Rei de Ouro, one Lt. Hilário Jovino Pereira, was unfazed by this intimidating audience, or at least so he said in a 1931 interview, explaining that "in Bahia, carnival groups [went] to pay their respects to the gov-ernor in the square in front of the palace."[34]

Well-intentioned defenders of "things Brazilian" have obviously exaggerated in saying that Brazilian popular music met only scorn and repression from the elite of turn-of-the-century Rio de Janeiro. They also exaggerated in saying that during the belle epoque gui-tars had disappeared completely from elite salons, to be replaced by pianos. Evidence of a more complex situation can be found in Lima Barreto's novel *The Sad End of Policarpo Quaresma* (1915), which begins with a chapter titled "The Guitar Lesson." The hero of the novel is Major Policarpo, a respectable amateur scholar of middling social status. Policarpo's reading of "historians, chroniclers, and philosophers" has convinced him that the modinha with guitar accompaniment is "the poetic and musical expression characteristic of the national spirit" of Brazil.[35] The patriotic scholar therefore takes guitar lessons from a troubadour, Ricardo Coração dos Outros. Policarpo's neighbors vigorously reject the idea and declare him mad: "A guitar in such a respectable house!" they exclaim. "A serious man involved in low-life stuff like that!" Policarpo defends himself on nationalist grounds: "It is prejudice to suppose that every man who plays the guitar lacks social decency. The modinha is the most genuine expression of our national poetry, and the guitar is the instrument that it requires." The patriotic Major Policarpo mobilizes historical facts and foreign authorities to buttress his point. "It is we who have abandoned the genre, but it has held a place of honor, in Lisbon during the last century, with Father Caldas [Barbosa] who had an audience of noble ladies. Beckford, a notable Englishman, praised him highly."[36]

The problem is knowing the referent of that "we" who had supposedly abandoned the modinha. Other passages in the same novel make clear that it was by no means everyone in Rio de Janeiro. The humble troubadour Ricardo Coração dos Outros appears as "an artist who honored, with his frequent presence, the best families" of certain distant neighborhoods of the city. Furthermore, he aspired to sing in posh neighborhoods. "His fame was already reaching São Cristóvão and soon (he hoped) Botafogo would invite him, because the newspapers already mentioned his name and discussed his poetic achievements."[37] The novel also describes a gathering at the house of one of Policarpo's respectable neighbors — a general, no less. The general's guests gave a cold reception to an Italian air sung by a talented young conservatory graduate but enthusiastically celebrated the modinhas and guitar work of Ricardo Coração dos Outros. The description shows contradictory social impulses: lip service to proprieties that condemned Carioca popular culture, along with warm applause for some of its everyday manifestations. Here are the diverse reactions of a heterogeneous society and attitudes that vary according to the particular situation or group in which people find themselves. The career of this fictional troubadour has much in common with that of Catulo da Paixão Cearense, except that Catulo accomplished what Ricardo only dreamed of: the artistic conquest of prestigious Botafogo.

By the time of his performance at the presidential palace, Catulo was combining northeastern *sertanejo* ("country") music with his earlier, more urbane modinhas. A later chronicler praised him for helping rehabilitate "popular, native song, belittled by anti-national prejudice."[38] But this nationalist tone did not imply a condemnation of foreign styles. European and U.S. rhythms were not swept aside to make way for sertanejo music from northeastern Brazil. To the contrary, the hits of the 1900 carnival season prominently included polkas of various kinds, often in hybrid forms (combined with Brazilian rhythms like lundu or the Cuban-derived habanera), and carnival balls featured waltzes, masurkas, quadrilles, and schottisches as well.[39] That kind of international diversity in popular carnival music continued to reign for decades, becoming ever more eclectic and eventually including U.S. pop music, especially jazz and the Charleston. Tinhorão reports that "the greatest hit of the 1916 Carioca carnival was the one-step 'Caraboo,' by the Jamaican Sam Marshall," only thinly disguised as a Brazilian carnival march.[40] Clearly, during Rio's belle epoque an interest in Brazilian popular culture did not contradict an interest in the latest international vogue.

Nor was a mixture of such interests exactly a novelty in Brazil. The lundu, for example, was derived from the rhythm of *batuque*, the dance of African slaves, but its choreography "largely imitated the Spanish dance called fandango."[41] A fusion of lundu and polka had occurred not long after French traveling musical theater companies introduced the polka in the mid-1840s. Tinhorão calls lundu's vigorous successor, the Brazilian maxixe, "the nationalized version of the polka imported from Europe."[42] It emerged in the 1870s and eventually found acceptance among the Carioca elite, whereupon it returned to Europe as the new "dance of the moment," causing a commotion in Paris. The cultural heterogeneity of the artistic world at this time made possible events like the 1892 performance of a Spanish actress, Pepa Ruíz, who appeared "dressed as a Bahiana, singing a 'tango' entitled *Munguzá*."[43] The "tango" with the African sounding name was really a maxixe. As we will see, maxixe was to have a decisive influence in the invention of samba.

Maxixes were often called tangos: another demonstration of the fluidity of musical genres in the period. Until very recently, Brazilian musical groups did not specialize in any specific rhythm. As late as the 1950s, the orchestras that performed live on Brazilian National Radio into the 1950s presented sambas along with mambos and boleros. In the late nineteenth century, the *choro* string bands of Rio played maxixes but also waltzes. The bands that provided music for carnival in the early twentieth century played fox-trots, maxixes, and *toadas sertanejas* ("country music") along with their carnival marches. Catulo da Paixão Cearense's sensational toada sertaneja of 1912, *Cabocla di Caxangá* (roughly "Country Girl from Caxangá"), inspired a carnival parade group with a regionalist motif the following year. The parading group included João Pernambuco (co-author, with Catulo, of "*Cabocla di Caxangá*") as well as Donga and Pixinguinha (fourteen years before their meeting with Gilberto Freyre). Grupo de Caxangá, they called themselves. Dressed as bandit followers of the famous outlaw Antonio Silvino, a sort of Robin Hood of the Brazilian backlands, the group frolicked through the streets of the capital performing an eclectic musical repertory including, but not limited to, northeastern folk themes.[44]

Having established the link between popular music and the Brazilian elite, we can begin to see how the elite's musical tastes related to their other concerns. Our example will be the writer Afonso Arinos, a schoolmate of Prudente de Moraes at the prestigious Pedro II Secondary School. Arinos was also a friend of Catulo da Paixão Cearense, who considered him "truly immortal because of his works on the life and customs of the northeastern backlander." According to Catulo, "Arinos was a lover of everything Brazilian. Nature bewitched him. It seemed that his very blood was the sap of the brazilwood tree."[45] Afonso Arinos was also warmly remembered by the sambista Donga, who, in later years described to his daughter the house he had shared in the early 1910s with Pixinguinha and Heitor dos Prazeres, another early sambista, in downtown Rio. Recalled Donga:

Even though it was old and run-down . . . we felt set up and liked our new place. People like Catulo da Paixão Cearense, Olegário Mariano, Bastos Tigre, Hermes Fontes, Medeiros de Albuquerque, Edmundo Bittencourt, Emílio de Meneses, Gutemberg Cruz, and the great Dr. Afonso Arinos de Mello Franco, then president of the Brazilian Academy of Letters, came to visit us there. [Afonso Arinos] thought so much of us that he always invited us to perform at his residence in Botafogo and at his country estate in Tombadouro, where Catulo composed the sertaneja song "The Deer Ate the Tenderest Grass."[46]

Arinos's association with relatively obscure popular musicians—Donga and Pixinguinha being still far from their future celebrity—is an unexplored aspect of his life, not mentioned in standard biographical sources.[47]

The musical "relations" of Afonso Arinos make him a kind of precursor of the (some would say schizophrenic) attitude of modernist Brazilian intellectuals like Freyre, divided between an interest in things cosmopolitan and an attraction to things Brazilian. These divergent concerns do not necessarily need to be reconciled as parts of a coherent ideology. Rather than a creator of cultural syntheses, an intellectual like Arinos can be better viewed as another of our cultural mediators, moving between and bringing into contact various "worlds," leaving his tracks in all of them, and sometimes opening them to other outsiders in the process. What else could have been his intention when he staged a traditional folk dance pageant like "bumba-meu-boi" in the Municipal Theater of São Paulo?[48] What else did he have in mind when he gave a dance to mark the conclusion of a series of lectures on Brazilian legends and traditions, surprising his elegant guests with a presentation of cateretê by "authentic" rural people from the interior?[49]

Though associated with São Paulo, Arinos was born in Minas

Gerais in 1868, the son of an imperial senator, and grew up in the interior of the country. When he was nine, the family moved to Vila Boa do Anhangüera, then capital of the remote province of Goiás, where he lived until 1881. Eventually, however, he attended the prestigious São Paulo law school, where one of his classmates was Paulo Prado, future author of *Portrait of Brazil* and a millionaire who would one day finance many of the activities of the Brazilian modernists, including the visits of Blaise Cendrars to Rio de Janeiro, São Paulo, and Minas Gerais. Arinos's modernism is especially intriguing in a man known for his monarchist sentiments during the first years of the republic. His polished manners impressed his friends, according to one biographer, Tristão de Athayde. Another (his nephew) describes Arinos as "elegant and open-handed." After graduating from law school, young Arinos moved to São João Del Rey, in western Minas Gerais, where he began to write the short stories of *Pelo sertão* (*Through the Backlands*), an early landmark of Brazilian literary regionalism. His subjects were rivermen and the characteristic landscape of western Minas Gerais, described in a manner that attempted to be faithful to local language. Arinos traveled constantly back and forth between his home in the central Brazilian countryside, where he sometimes camped out with the cowboys to hear their stories and songs, and various more cosmopolitan destinations. His habitual itinerary included Belo Horizonte (the state capital), Rio, São Paulo, even Paris. In Paris, he socialized with the Brazilian royal family. In Rio, he consorted with some of the most distinguished Brazilian men of letters, including Machado de Assis, but also with Catulo da Paixão Cearense, Donga, and Pixinguinha.

Tristão de Athayde identifies a "contradictory tendency" in the life and work of Afonso Arinos, the pull of "diverging polarities" between *cosmo* and *regio*. Here is the drama, not just of Afonso Arinos, but of the whole Brazilian nationality, "and generally that of all recent nationalities."[50] Athayde describes the individual, psychological reflections of the great national drama in persons such as Afonso Arinos as a struggle between two libidos: "the concupiscence of the wide world and the concupiscence of the homeland."[51] Hence the "itinerate" life of this cultural mediator. Writes Athayde:

"Arinos lived overseas, or more precisely, on the road, because of the passion for the unknown that he felt within him." Hence his literary attempts to "escape a narrow regionalism that leads to secessions and prejudices."[31]

Gilberto Freyre, another cosmopolitan regionalist, had the same preoccupations. Freyre described Arinos fondly in a 1924 newspaper article: "Arinos was like a letter always in the mail, not misplaced, not spindled as undeliverable because addressed to a deceased person or bearing the name of a town no longer in existence. Rather, Arinos was a letter permanently traveling back and forth, always returning to the sender, who merely darkened the lightly penciled address and remailed it. And the 'sender' was the *pequena pátria* [the home locality] that would not let him go but could not completely satisfy him." Freyre asks himself: "Is not all purely artistic vocation like a misaddressed letter or telegram in a Brazil like the Brazil of today?"[53]

In 1900, Afonso Arinos published a small book, *A unidade da pátria* (The Unity of the Nation), today almost forgotten. It attempted to examine all these contradictions—between foreign and native, between the refined and the rustic, between the motion of travel and the permanence of tradition. A look at that book will open our discussion of the problem of unity and diversity in Brazilian society.

4 The Unity of the Nation

Afonso Arinos is generally classified as a regionalist writer, but he did not promote centrifugal regionalism in Brazil. In fact, *A unidade da pátria* was written to exorcise the specter of radical regionalization. In that book, Arinos says clearly that "Brazil is so regionalized that, in order that the provinces not be totally foreign to each other, a great effort is needed to strengthen the moral unity of the nation."[1] His interest in "things Brazilian" was directly linked to his preoccupation with the problem of national unity. And within the culture of the common folk, popular music occupied a special place for Arinos: "[A] great anonymous power—almost subterranean, so to speak, like the action of the water table in the formation the riverbank—configures the cultural fabric of our nationality, with its common legends and traditions, flying from South to North and from North to South on the shimmering wings of popular song."[2] The itinerant Arinos placed little value on the notion of Brazilian communities narrowly rooted and enclosed in regional traditions. He esteemed the mixture of those traditions that, in their "anonymous" and "subterranean" workings, created the unity of Brazil. For that reason, Arinos admired the boatmen and cattle drovers who crisscrossed the territory of Brazil. He prized the migrant from the arid northeast who went to tap rubber trees in the Amazonian rain forest and esteemed the Bahian migrant who labored in the coffee fields of São Paulo and learned to play southern forms of Afro-Brazilian folk music. Arinos attributed what cultural unity Brazil possessed to the *povo*, the common people, "unjustly called indolent" and relatively superior "in morality to the upper classes." "The common people do what they can," he proclaimed, "and no more should be expected of them."[3] Arinos lamented the fall of the monarchy and the creation of a loosely federated United States of Brazil in 1889. He campaigned for a unifying alliance between the elite and the povo:

"The duty to ally for action falls all the more on the well-educated classes since, until now, the unity of Brazil has been maintained not by the superior sort, but by the common people."[4]

Afonso Arinos believed in the power of popular culture to configure a national identity. In other words, he was a cultural nationalist. At this point, a brief exploration of the phenomenon of cultural nationalism—which differs substantially from country to country—will provide useful perspective on the Brazilian case.

In theoretical terms, most scholars now agree that a "national consciousness" is not a natural and primordial, but rather a socially constructed and fairly recent, phenomenon—a distinctively modern way of viewing the world, in fact. Eric Hobsbawm endorses Ernest Gellner's description of the process whereby national identities arise. "With Gellner, I would stress the element of artifact, invention, and social engineering which enters into the making of nations," writes Hobsbawm, and he goes on to quote Gellner as follows: "Nations as a natural, God-given way of classifying men, as an inherent though long-delayed political destiny, are a myth; nationalism, which sometimes takes pre-existing cultures and turns them into nations, sometimes invents them, and often obliterates pre-existing cultures: That is a reality."[5] "In short," continues Hobsbawm, "for the purposes of analysis, nationalism comes before nations. Nations do not make states and nationalisms, but the other way around."[6] Benedict Anderson, using different words to convey a similar idea, describes a nation as an "imagined political community . . . imagined as both inherently limited and sovereign."[7] According to Anderson, "All communities larger than primordial villages of face-to-face contact (and perhaps even these) are imagined. Communities are to be distinguished not by their falsity/genuineness, but by the style in which they are imagined."[8] The nation-state vogue, in Anderson's estimation, began in the late eighteenth century and became the international norm of legitimate political organization only at the end of World War I, with the creation of the League of Nations. Immanuel Wallerstein gives a slightly different periodization that likewise emphasizes the modern advent of nationalism: "A world consisting of these nation-states came into existence even partially only in the six-teenth century. Such a world was theorized and became a matter of widespread consciousness even later, only in the nineteenth cen-tury. It became an inescapably universal phenomenon later still, in fact only after 1945." [9] By this timetable, Brazil's post-1930 nation-alism was right on schedule.

Hobsbawm, Gellner, and Anderson agree that a nation is a sym-bolic construct.[10] Before the eighteenth century, most European societies were governed through an entirely different kind of sym-bol: principally royal lineages that "derived their prestige, aside from any aura of divinity, from, shall we say, miscegenation, be-cause [cross-dynastic alliances] were signs of a superordinate sta-tus." [11] The nobility did not belong to a single "people" or "nation." Aristocracies did not treasure the notion of national purity nor the idea of belonging to a single piece of "native soil." In reference to this aristocratic mentality, Georg Simmel emphasizes the "in-consequentiality of political and geographic boundaries compared to that which is common to all nobles simply because they are nobles." [12] The international quality of royal dynasties—the Bour-bons, for example—is quite well-known. Simmel points out that the same phenomenon operated throughout the European aris-tocracy:

> Many families of high noble status in European countries have foreign origins. In England, the Fitzgeralds and the Duke of Leicester come from Florence, the Dukes of Portland from Hol-land. In France, the Broglies come from Piedmont, the Dukes of Cars from Perurgia, the Luynes from Arezzo. In Austria, the Clarys come from Florence. In Prussia, the Lynars come from Faenza. In Poland, the Poniatowskis come from Bologna. In Italy, the Roccas come from Croatia, the Ruspolis from Scot-land, the Torlonias from France, and so on.[13]

In the contrary case, a homogeneous nobility could give stability to ethnically diverse political groupings, such as the Austro-Hungarian Empire. The aristocratic disregard for the geographic origin in the makeup of political alliances was mirrored, to a degree, in the anti-aristocratic politics of the French Revolution, which made the English polemicist Thomas Paine a member of the French National Assembly.[14] Aristocrats and anti-aristocrats alike privileged ideology over ethnicity. But the growing importance of nationalism in the nineteenth century rooted political legitimacy almost invariably in the idea of national community, and community usually implied commonality. Commonality, in turn, was most often imagined as ethnic homogeneity. Because human populations are, in fact, generally heterogeneous, a sense of homogeneity had to be created. Ethnic homogeneity became a nationalist project.

Imagining nations involved imagining a shared past: the location of ethnic roots, repository of a national essence. But the idea of a national essence, rooted in "time immemorial," runs counter to "the essentially dynamic and often hybrid nature of cultures."[15] Thus, to return to a concept mentioned in Chapter 1, the imagining of national roots necessitates, in Richard Peterson's words, "the fabrication of authenticity." This preoccupation with national authenticity arose, apparently, in eighteenth-century Germany— principally in the thought of the poet and philosopher Johann Gottfried Herder.

Herder was reacting against the Francophilia of the Prussian nobility of his day. He opposed the French concept of civilization (which "emphasizes what is common to all human beings, or should be") with the German concept Kultur (which stresses "national difference and the particular identity of groups"). Herder criticized the French culture as superficial, false, and immoral and, in contrast, praised the simple but virtuous culture of common Germans, collectively "the people" (precisely what Arinos meant by povo).[16] This emphasis on the common people and their customs as repositories of the Volksgeist or Nationalgeist—the authentic "national spirit"—explains the nationalist interest in folklore and popular culture. The Brazilian celebration of samba, then, is only one example of a widespread phenomenon.

Purity and authenticity go together in this "essentializing" conceptualization of a national spirit. Each people's national essence, the untainted wellspring of collective identity, is supposedly unique and not to be plagiarized or mixed. More recent scholarship has shown conclusively that interethnic mixing lies at the origin of all cultures, even the oldest and seemingly "purest." Still, the essentialist view continues to shape the basic assumptions undergirding most cultural nationalism and must be kept in mind for that reason.

The present analysis, on the other hand, rejects the idea of a pure or authentic *national* culture along with the idea of a pure or authentic *popular* culture. There will be no attempt here to define what is authentic "popular culture" (as opposed to "mass culture" or "hegemonic culture"), to gauge its purity, or to locate its authentic repositories. Instead, I assume constant cultural interaction among multiplicitous social groups, resulting in the phenomenon known as transculturation.

The concept of transculturation gained currency from the work of the Cuban anthropologist Fernando Ortiz. In 1940, Ortiz published *Cuban Counterpoint of Tobacco and Sugar* with an enthusiastic preface by Bronislaw Malinowski. The following passage from Malinowski's preface sums up the concept of transculturation: "It is a process in which something is always given in exchange for what is received. It is a 'give-and-take' . . . modifying each side of the equation, a process from which a new—compound and complex—reality emerges, a reality that is not a mechanical aggregate of characteristics, nor even a mosaic, but rather a new, original, and independent phenomenon."[17] The Brazilian appropriation of U.S. funk music provides a recent example. Urban Brazilians took the U.S. music but gave it meanings of their own, used it in an entirely different way.[18] In addition, transculturation occurs not only internationally but also among culturally diverse groups in the same society. As we have seen, an intense cultural give-and-take has characterized the relationship between the Brazilian elite and popular classes for centuries.

This kind of transculturation—the sort that resulted in the transformation of samba into a Brazilian national emblem—inevitably accompanied the racial mixing that Gilberto Freyre tried to make into a new definition of Brazilian authenticity during the 1930s. Néstor García Canclini applies the term "hybrid" to cover "diverse intercultural mixes—not only the racial ones" usually indicated by the term "mestiçagem." [19] Freyre used the term "hybrid" in the same way. He hoped that, given the diverse racial and cultural origins of Brazilian society, a focus on hybridity might provide the new basis for Brazilian unity.

Unity and diversity had been among Brazil's gravest political challenges since colonial times. The responses had alternated, over the course of our history, between centralizing and decentralizing political initiatives, sometimes in odd combination. One can interpret the rise of samba as a national music (with the accompanying transformation of a particular variant of popular culture into a national culture) as one of those initiatives. Let us take a rapid bird's-eye view of the theme of Brazilian unity and diversity over several centuries to bring everything back in the end (as the reader doubtless suspects) to samba.

José Murilo de Carvalho cites an interesting description of colonial Brazil by the early nineteenth-century French traveler Auguste de Saint Hilaire. Saint Hilaire noted that the various Brazilian provinces "rarely communicate with each other and often are mutually ignorant of each others' existence." He added that "there is no common center in Brazil." [20] This is what Raimundo Faoro called the tendency toward "centrifugal dismemberment" that resulted, after Brazilian independence (1822), in a "disperse, disarticulated, and fluid nation." [21] Hence the difficulty of many interpreters in explaining why Brazil remained territorially unified while Spanish America fragmented politically in the postindependence period.

Because of the Napoleonic invasion of Portugal in 1807, João VI (still officially regent, rather than king, until the death of his demented mother) moved the Portuguese royal court to Rio de Janeiro. This move had a clearly centralizing impact, whether or not that was what the soon-to-be king had in mind. Years passed, and Napoleon was defeated, but still the king lingered in Rio. In 1820, Portugal underwent a liberal revolution that challenged the king's right to keep the royal court outside of Europe. In order to weaken the position of Rio, the national assembly of Portugal (the Côrtes) encouraged the political decentralization of Brazil. Whether or not they recognized the authority of the Côrtes, the regional elite of the

Brazilian provinces embraced decentralization as a blow against the Rio-based royal bureaucracy.

Thus, the events leading to independence in 1822 did not flow from a well-defined project of national unification. Emília Viotti da Costa shows that neither the various unsuccessful anticolonial rebellions (many of them strongly regionalist in character), nor the political movement that finally did achieve independence, were born of nationalist preoccupations. For example, the architects of the 1792 conspiracy in the Brazilian capital harbored hopes that revolutionary France might somehow take over Rio de Janeiro. Carvalho agrees that "the provincial independence movements of the late eighteenth and early nineteenth centuries all had republican tendencies and did not care much about unity." [22] The elite of central Brazil clung to the idea of retaining links with Portugal and refused to proclaim independence until the last possible moment. According to Costa, "The conditions that led to national integration and inspired nationalist ideas in Europe were lacking in Brazil," and as a consequence, "the maintenance of Brazil's territorial integrity after independence . . . cannot be attributed to a strong nationalist ideology: Brazilian elites simply recognized that the only way to assure the independent status of the nation was to eschew secession." [23] Therefore, only after formal independence from Portugal did Brazilians turn their attention to projects of national integration.

Pedro I, the first ruler of the independent Brazilian empire, was a centralizer, so his abdication in 1831 can be interpreted as an early failure of centralization.[24] The regency that followed the abdication of Pedro I saw the revival of centrifugal currents, often inspired by the federal model of the United States. The regent Diogo Feijó, for instance, promulgated measures that enhanced the autonomy of the provinces. And it was the symbol of the crown, rather than the idea of nation, according to Ludwig Lauerhass Jr., that Brazilians continued to view as the best guarantee of unity against territorial disintegration.[25] Following the regency, the monarchy remained the primary stay of political stability during the half-century reign of Pedro II over his more "cosmopolitan" than nationalist empire.

With the arrival of the Republic in 1889, the symbol of the nation had to substitute for the crown in giving legitimacy to the new rulers. Now unity could be achieved only by comprehending "the essence of Brazil" and putting it at the center of a nationalist movement. Comprehending the national essence became the goal of a relatively small first generation of nationalist intellectuals, active between 1880 and 1914, who did not become directly involved in politics. One was Sílvio Romero, already mentioned in connection with the Carioca elite's miniature folk revival at the turn of the century. Romero argued against the European immigrant colonies then forming in the southern region of the country, precisely on the grounds of the threat they supposedly posed to national unity. Euclides da Cunha was another who spoke of a divided country in his famous account of the 1890s millenarian movement in the northeastern backlands. Alberto Torres, the influential essayist, considered the lack of unity one of our greatest problems as a nation. His comment that Brazil would have to "create its own nationality artificially" shows an early awareness of the process by which identities could be constructed.[26] Among his suggestions for unification was the creation of a centralized "coordinating power" represented by delegates at the state, municipal, and district levels. Torres also suggested that the name Federative Republic of Brazil replace the more plural sounding name of United States of Brazil.

The tension between centralizing and decentralizing currents created confusing situations in republican political practice. Federalism (frequently drawing inspiration from the North American example and invoking democratic principles) was used on a number of occasions to ward off dictatorship at the national level. For example, federative democracy was the argument used by Rui Barbosa against the "Jacobinism" of the Republic's second military president, Floriano Peixoto. Nevertheless, most of the time decentralization redounded to the benefit of local and regional oligarchies, whose goals were hardly democratic and who were willing to adopt any maneuver that increased their own power.

The narrow regional orientation of these oligarchies brought trouble. The economic activities of the various regions of Brazil were ill-coordinated at the national level and generally oriented toward the international market. "From an economic point of view," in the words of Boris Fausto, "national integration was fragile during the empire and it remained fragile during the republic."[27] The republican constitution of 1891 went so far as to assure Brazilian states the right to contract foreign debts without the mediation of any financial institution at the national level. During the great coffee boom of the late nineteenth and early twentieth centuries, the coffee-cultivating oligarchy of the states of São Paulo and Minas Gerais impeded the formation of parties that might represent national currents of political opinion. They were merely playing it safe, though, because national currents of public opinion hardly existed yet. Furthermore, the coffee oligarchy expressed its preference for a certain kind of workforce. As Octávio Ianni puts it: "With the abolition of slavery and the proclamation of the republic, state power passed into the hands of the coffee oligarchy, which already had begun to depend on European immigrant labor. In the eyes of that oligarchy, Indians, blacks, even Brazilian whites took second place, and immigrants became prized."[28]

A movement to end this oligarchy's hegemony over the rest of Brazil began because of demands by various groups not linked to the coffee economy, including urban middle classes and reformist junior army officers referred to collectively as the *tenentes*, or lieutenants.[29] During the late 1920s, these groups came together in a Liberal Alliance—founded on an accord among leaders from non-coffee-producing states as widely separated as Paraíba (in the northeast) and Rio Grande do Sul (in the far south)—that managed to propel Getúlio Vargas to the presidency of the republic as a result of the revolution of 1930. The geographically dispersed origins of the alliance and its common denominator in regional economies not founded on coffee lead Lauerhass to argue that the movement of 1930 had formed "principally in response to regional, rather than nationalist, discontents." Nevertheless, because of its social and regional heterogeneity and its lack of a unifying ideology, the Liberal Alliance needed national organizing principles to undergird its political strategies.[30] Never had the spirit of national unity been so important to a Brazilian regime. Protesting the "threat of dictatorship," political forces in São Paulo once again turned to federalist ideas, but the victors of 1930 managed to hold them in check, and they even burned state flags on various occasions. It was amid this conflictive atmosphere, in 1933, that Gilberto Freyre published *The Masters and the Slaves*, with its positive evaluation of racial mixing as Brazil's distinctive national characteristic; and it was in these years, too, that samba became consolidated as the "national music."

In the wake of the 1930 revolution, the dominant political and cultural movements of Brazil became overwhelmingly centralizing, unifying, and homogenizing—in a word, nationalizing. Admittedly, each one of those constituent processes contained its own complexities, yet the overall progressive thrust is clear and contradicts the assertion of Carlos Guilherme Motta, who attributes the vogue of "things Brazilian" to a kind of aristocratic nostalgia: "Works like *The Masters and the Slaves*, produced by a son of the Old Republic, indicate efforts to comprehend Brazilian reality on the part of an aristocratic elite that was already losing power. Their loss of social and political power inspired a backward gaze, a search for lost times, a return to roots."[31] To the contrary, Freyre's famous book was part of an intellectual project quite in tune with the political tenor of the revolutionary 1930s. Freyre's regionalism was entirely as nationalist as the regionalism of Afonso Arinos. It did not represent a return to roots so much as an imaginative recreation of those roots. Lúcia Lippi de Oliveira argues that "the authoritarian government [principally of the period 1937–45] so forcefully assured centralization that regionalist manifestations no longer threatened the whole." And she goes on to say that "none of the regional models was chosen to represent Brazil as a whole."[32]

Under the authoritarian umbrella a new model of national authenticity was fabricated in post-1930 Brazil. Various cultural elements (a typical costume here, a dance rhythm there) were selected from the already existing regional models and recombined to form a homogenizing official national culture. As we will see, the popular culture of urban Rio de Janeiro predominated in the mix. The "national dish," for example, is made from the black beans eaten in Rio rather than from the *mulatinho* beans eaten in the northeast. Before examining the construction of that national model, however, we must inquire how the problem of national unity intersected with the debate over race mixture that had for so long preoccupied the intellectual inventors of Brazilian national identity.

5 Race Mixture

By the end of the nineteenth century, intellectuals had combined the debate over Brazilian national identity—or national disunity—with the problem of Brazil's "backwardness" when compared with Europe, the principal point of reference for evolutionist thinking then dominant. A defeatist attitude revealed itself in the very framing of the question: Why are we backward? Finding an answer required the discovery of what made us different from Europeans, and thus "worse." In this view, our national identity contained, from the outset, the contamination of a mysterious racial or perhaps climatically determined "illness" destined to place us at a disadvantage vis-à-vis the rest of the world. Brazilian national identity had to be discovered in order to be cured.

The mestiço, or person of mixed race (primarily African and European in the case of Brazil), became the scapegoat of Brazilian backwardness. Despite the countercurrents we have traced in earlier chapters, it must be admitted that turn-of-the-century intellectuals generally looked with scorn on the same bean dishes and musical precursors of samba that would, in later decades, become the objects of proud preservationist efforts. Gilberto Freyre's great feat was to provide a positive theoretical color for mestiço culture, defining "things Brazilian" as a combination—partly harmonious, partly conflictive—of African, Portuguese, and indigenous traits, the product of a historical encounter between "the big house and the slave quarters," to quote the title of his influential book, published in English as *The Masters and the Slaves*. According to Freyre, racially mixed Brazilian culture was not the cause of Brazilian backwardness but, to the contrary, something to be carefully nurtured, the very guarantee of our distinctiveness among nations and the mark of our destiny—which was to be increasingly mestiço.

Without forgetting the pioneering aspects of Freyre's thought, we should not neglect the previous existence of a Brazilian intellectual tradition devoted to the study of race and mestiço culture. The interest in folklore has already been discussed. Museums, geographic institutes, and medical and law schools had seen an interminable debate over Brazilian racial types. According to Lília Schwarcz, "men of science" inside and outside Brazil pointed to the country as "a unique and singular case of extreme miscegenation" and viewed race mixing as the central issue affecting our national destiny.[1] Rather than mechanically applying European racist theories, Schwarcz shows that "local elites consumed that type of literature, but made original adaptations" to the Brazilian case.[2] "By picking and choosing what worked and discarding what seemed too problematic," they fashioned an "original copy" of the racist doctrines then in vogue internationally.[3] In the process, Brazilian intellectuals even relativized the term "race" itself: "Rather than a closed, physical, natural concept, [race] was understood as an object of knowledge, the meaning of which would be constantly renegotiated and tested in that specific historical context with so much invested in biological modes of analysis."[4]

An example of this original adaptation of European ideas is the Brazilian reinterpretation of the "decadent" French thinker Joseph Arthur de Gobineau, a personal friend of Pedro II. Gobineau had produced, in the words of Tzvetan Todorov, "a profoundly pessimistic philosophy of history," in which "a tragic paradox weighed over all humanity." Gobineau condemned race mixing as a universally degenerative force that inevitably weakened the races involved, but his thought did not stop there. The "tragic paradox" was that every racially pure human tribe necessarily had to mix with others in order to become civilized. The road to civilization, then, led also to perdition. No culture was exempt from the quandary: either remain pure and savage or undergo enervating amalgamation. Both paths led to destruction. "Mixture, mixture everywhere, always mixture," wrote Gobineau, "behold the clearest, most guaranteed, most durable work of great societies and powerful civilizations."[5] Todorov summarizes the logical consequences of the paradox: "When a society becomes strong enough, it tends to subjugate others, but by doing so it risks its identity and loses its strength." In other words (also Todorov's), "every demonstration of power becomes a guarantee of frailness, each success, a step toward failure."[6]

What, then, of Brazilian society? Already racially mixed without becoming powerful—should it abandon all hope of achieving civilization? Some Brazilian authors did not bow their heads to Gobineau's pessimism but instead appropriated the portions of this thought that interested them and discarded the rest, to create a much more optimistic vision. This was the case of Graça Aranha, a former professor of the important Recife law school, whose "poliphonic" naturalist novel *Canaã* (1901) explored notions of race.

Canaã describes the adventures and dialogues of two German immigrants, Milkau and Lentz, who resolved to begin new lives as agricultural colonists in the Brazilian state of Espíritu Santo. Lentz represents a pessimism that Aranha attributed to Nietzsche, while Milkau represents strains of Gobineau's thought, transformed by an almost Franciscan spirit of benign optimism. The two characters' dialogue on the subject of tropical forests reveals contrasting worldviews. Lentz sees the triumph of natural selection, in which "each beauty costs many deaths." Milkau, on the other hand, sees in the natural exuberance of the forest an "incessant permutation," in which "everything contributes to everything else" and each tree bestows a "portion of love" upon the whole.[7] Milkau's vision has evident consequences for the conceptualization of human races: "One of the errors committed by interpreters of history lies in the aristocratic prejudice of their idea of race. But no one has yet been able to define race, much less specify how one race can be distinguished from the others." Milkau's conclusion, without its festive tone, might have been written by Gobineau: "Races become civilized through fusion. In the encounter between advanced and virgin or savage races lies the conserving respite, the miracle that rejuvenates civilizations."[8]

The optimistic implications of Milkau's argument distance the character's thinking from Gobineau and move it in the direction of Freyre, as when, later in the novel, Milkau says that Brazil would have remained "a collection of chaste and separate races" were it not for "the strong and imperious sensuality of the conquerors" that took it upon themselves to form "that intermediate race . . . that binds the nation together."[9] Ultimately, however, Milkau's future projections veer toward a theory of "whitening" for the Brazilian population. "In the remote future," he explains, "the epoch of the mulatos will pass away, replaced by the age of new whites." According to José Paulo Paes, *Canaã* reveals its "eminently premodernist character" by recognizing the participation of "savage, virgin races in the civilizing process, although attributing to them a dependent and passive role."[10] Paes finds the utopian vision of *Canaã* not far distant from the later modernist nationalism called Anthropophagy, "with its strategy of cultural ingestion and its dream of a Carib Revolution."[11]

Graça Aranha's thinking was closer yet to that of Sílvio Romero, another Brazilian author who freely reinterpreted Gobineau. Romero participated actively in debates concerning race and national development, taking positions that often distance him from the eugenics advocated by many Brazilian writers and scientists.[12] Thales de Azevedo affirms that, from the mid-nineteenth century until the 1930s, the specter of race mixture furnished "an explanation of defects and weaknesses for a society at once optimistic and a bit dubious about the qualities of its common people."[13] Romero did not necessarily think more highly of the Brazilian people than did the intellectual exponents of eugenics, but like Aranha's fictional Milkau, Romero glimpsed a "better" future characterized by a general whitening, rather than degeneration, of the population. Romero's reflections start from the simple premise that, like it or not, the Brazilian people are of mixed race. "It avails us little, for now, to argue over whether this is good or bad," he wrote. "It is a fact, and that is enough."[14] And he did not view this as an exclusively Brazilian characteristic, "because people have mixed since primordial times," pointing out that areas of more recent settlement differed only because they were more easily "caught in the act" of miscegenation.[15] Countries like Brazil had the obligation to study the problem carefully and the right to propose their own solutions.

Roberto Ventura summarizes Romero's ideas in the following manner: "His theory of miscegenation and whitening begins from

assumptions that are partly racist (postulating the existence of in-
nate ethnic differences) and partly evolutionist (anticipating the
survival of the fittest). He predicted that whites would be victorious
in the 'struggle among races' and that their evolutionary superiority would guarantee their predominance in the process of race
mixing. As a result, he foresaw the total whitening of the Brazilian population in three or four centuries."[16] As a literary critic,
Romero joined this theory of whitening to his vision of race mixing as Brazil's "factor of national differentiation." That differentiation constituted an extremely important element in his nationalist
attacks on "mimesis," or imitation of foreign literatures.[17] Therefore, even while condemning Brazilians as inferior, Sílvio Romero
could affirm that "each Brazilian is a mestiço, if not in blood, in his
ideas."[18] Race mixture was, in Romero's view, our only guarantee
of creating nonimitative art.

Theories of progressive race mixture were shared by various
other Brazilian intellectuals — for example, Joaquim Nabuco, Afrânio Peixoto, and João Batista Lacerda[19] — none of whom, however,
approximated the future enthusiasm of Gilberto Freyre. Unlike
Freyre, they did not value race mixing for its own sake. To the
contrary, they mistrusted it, accepting it only in the absence of
something better. Even the first studies of folklore carried out in
Brazil, including the work of Sílvio Romero, return frequently to
the notion of the "poverty" of Brazilian popular traditions.[20] Race
mixture was Brazil's only mark of uniqueness, but it did not necessarily signify cultural richness or vigor — until the work of Gilberto
Freyre.

One of Romero's most important contributions to later intellectual generations was his passionate criticism of nineteenth-century
Brazilian romanticism with its glorification of the Indian. Romantic writers such as José de Alencar, like their European counter-
parts, had gone in search of national roots during the middle of the
century, and they had employed indigenous characters as symbols
of Brazilian cultural purity.[21] According to Dante Moreira Leite,
"Literary Indianism . . . created a sort of Brazilian middle ages that
both met the aesthetic requirements of the day and gave some historical content to nationalism."[22] Alencar's figure of the "hand-

some, strong, and free" Indian brave had been modeled, as Alfredo Bosi demonstrates, "in combination with a frank apology for colonization," clearly symbolized in the submission of Alencar's famous indigenous character Peri to the charms of his white mistress.[23]

Romero radically altered the tenor of the Brazilian intellectual search for national authenticity by replacing the figure of the indigenous person with the person of mixed race as the primary symbol of Brazilian originality. Romero went so far as to state that "the Indian is not Brazilian."[24] Therefore, Romero categorically disqualified José de Alencar's project to create a national poetic tradition that would be "entirely Brazilian" because it was "inspired by the language of the savages."[25] Poetry in Tupi (the indigenous language most important in Brazilian history) was Tupi poetry, according to Romero, and not Brazilian poetry at all. In sum, Brazilian culture began with race mixing. "There can be but one source of nationality in Brazilian poetry," he wrote, "the genius, the true spirit of the people that emerges from the complex of our ethnic origins."[26]

Romero recognized the search for originality as the one great achievement of Romantic "Indianism," which he called "a battle cry to unite us and put us to work for ourselves literarily."[27] Romantic "Indianism" revealed the desire to find worth in certain aspects of tropicality, suggesting that a tropical civilization might be in some ways superior to European antecedents precisely because of its proximity to "exuberant" nature. Living in the tropics, which had long been regarded as an unmitigated disadvantage, here began to be transformed into a point of pride. Poems proliferated to sing the praises of tropical skies that "have more stars" and to criticize, by comparison, the chilly landscapes of Europe— "regions so dead, without enchantment or attraction," to paraphrase the verse of Gonçalves de Magalhães. Post-Romantic critics made the idea even more explicit. Already in 1888, Júnior Araripe championed the virtues of "the tropical environment and its ethnic and cultural mixture," contrasting an ardent Brazilian realism to European decadence. Here, then—twirling among the Romantics, Júnior Araripe, and Romero—we find the roots of Gilberto Freyre's

"Luso-tropicalism" of the second quarter of the twentieth century.

Because race mixture has never been a uniform phenomenon, its ideological exponents have always had to choose which sort of mixture fit the Brazilian national identity they had in mind. Euclides da Cunha, for example, never concealed his preference for the caboclo of the Brazilian interior (a mixture including traces of indigenous heritage) over the more black-and-white mixture typical of the coast. In part, da Cunha's choice represented a preference for a rural over an urban model, the countryside having long been considered the repository of folk authenticity and the coast being the location of most Brazilian cities. Similarly, Afonso Celso, in his 1900 book *Porque me ufano do meu país (Why I Am Proud of My Country)*—which became a standard text in Brazilian classrooms—excludes the mulato from his list of the country's racial types.[28] Nevertheless, during the early twentieth century, the mulato and the urban environment became increasingly central to debates over the origins of Brazilian identity. In the field of music, urban samba of Rio de Janeiro became the preeminent national symbol, while the *caipira* country music of São Paulo and the rural rhythms of the northeast became phenomena representing particular regions, rather than Brazil as a whole.

One should not, of course, look for an appreciation of the culture of people of mixed race in the bulk of Brazilian academic writing before *The Masters and the Slaves*. Even when criticizing the the assumptions of eugenics (as did Manuel Bomfim) scholars continued to regard people of mixed race as indolent, undisciplined, and shortsighted "because of poor upbringing." And the very pioneers of Afro-Brazilian studies did not hide their own racial prejudice, either. Raimundo Nina Rodrigues, the most famous of them, said that "the black race of Brazil . . . will always constitute one of the factors of our inferiority as a people." The historian Oliveira Vianna believed that blacks could never truly absorb, but only imitate, "Arian" culture. And Artur Ramos, in spite of affirming that the black race per se was not inferior, cited a "pre-logical mentality" in alleging the backwardness of black culture.[29]

On the other hand, one finds indication of a different attitude in the daily life of these same intellectuals—as, for example, when they formed friendships with popular musicians—and even more so in certain writers unrepresentative of the academic mainstream, like Afonso Arinos, Graça Aranha, and Lima Barreto. Another such writer, Alberto Torres, was later recognized as precursor by Gilberto Freyre himself. In a rare moment of modesty late in the 1950s, Freyre called Torres "perhaps the first Brazilian public writer to learn of Franz Boas's investigations on the nature of the relationship between race and physical and social environment."[30] In a similar vein, Freyre mentioned the pioneering work of Roquette Pinto, as well as ("here and there") Cândido Rondon, J. B. de Lacerda, José Veríssimo, Inglês de Souza, Afrânio Peixoto, Gilberto Amado, and ("with some lamentable lapses") Sílvio Romero and Euclides da Cunha.

The intellectual valorization of race mixing reflected a desire for national unity and homogeneity clearly evident in the debate over immigration that began in the mid-nineteenth century and reached its apogee in the late 1930s. According to Giralda Seyferth, the principal problem was how to transform immigrants into "real Brazilians." While immigrant leaders often argued for a cultural pluralism that would maintain even the distinct language of the newcomers, the opposing strategy was to champion "the ideal of national homogeneity to be achieved through assimilation and miscegenation."[31]

Immigration was prized by nationalists when it promised to "whiten" the population. Sílvio Romero, who looked forward (as we have seen) to the total whitening of Brazil, criticized German immigrants in the southern part of the country because they resisted mixing with the rest of the population. Brazil needed white immigrants who were willing to mix with Brazilians of color, and Romero resented seeing the Germans spurn "his people" as cultural and sexual partners. Romero thought we needed to Brazilianize the Germans so that they could whiten and civilize us—an almost anthropophagous approach.

Other immigrants were also assessed according to how they might contribute to this project of nationalist miscegenation. Undesirables (along with "segregationist" Germans) included all "backward" and "inferior" races. Africans were never considered among possible candidates for immigration. The Chinese were classified as "decadent" and "risky" (the risk being an "inappropriate" mixture). Japanese immigration became the topic of intense discussion, reaching venues as exalted as the national constituent assembly of 1934, the debate turning on whether or not the Japanese would mix racially.[32] The most coveted immigrants were Europeans, especially the people of southwestern Europe who, presumably, would mix most readily with the rest of the Brazilian population.

The project of forced assimilation and nationalization inspired a sharp reaction among some of the immigrants who resisted race mixing. Their racism and scorn for Brazil led Freyre to write a lecture titled "The Threatened Luso-Brazilian Culture," which will be discussed in the next chapter. Seyferth mentions articles published in the German-language press of Santa Catarina before the First World War that cited Gobineau and condemned Brazilian race mixing (calling it "ethnic chaos"). The Brazilian state strongly repressed these separatist or "pluralist" attitudes, especially after the revolution of 1930 made race mixing a semi-official doctrine. Article 121, Paragraph 6, of the 1934 constitution stipulated that "the entrance of immigrants into the national territory will be subject to the restrictions necessary to guarantee ethnic integration," and it created a quota system whereby immigrants of each nationality were annually not to exceed 2 percent of the total immigration from that country during the previous fifty years. Brazilian labor law of the period required that "no establishment may have more than one-third foreign employees."[33] "Ethnic integration," an official euphemism for race mixing, had become the policy of the authoritarian New State, declared by President Getúlio Vargas in 1937.

Giralda Seyferth affirms that "the New State . . . even though shifting to a dissembling rhetoric of racial democracy, had not abandoned the theory of whitening."[34] Nevertheless, another view of race mixing now competed with the notion of whitening, a view advanced principally by Gilberto Freyre, a view that gained rapid and enormous national popularity following the publication of The Masters and the Slaves in 1933. The race mixing envisioned by Freyre did not necessarily lead to the whitening of the nation. Instead, Freyre highlighted, in a very positive way, various "black" contributions to a miscegenated national culture. Freyre's vision, too, was a homogenizing one, often radically so, but it did not rest on an assumption of white superiority or the affirmation that the white race would dominate the "final mix." In Freyre's Brazil, the fact of race mixture would itself be a point of national pride. Let us see how he "invented" that pride.

6 Gilberto Freyre

The publication of *The Masters and the Slaves* was received immediately as a great event in the Brazilian intellectual world of the 1930s. Jorge Amado, the writer who practically created the Brazilian "mestiço" novel, remembers the event this way: "It was an explosion, a new fact of life, something like we had never had before, and right away there was a feeling that we had grown and become more capable. Nobody who didn't live through those times can know how beautiful it was."[1] Amado continues: "Gilberto's book dazzled the country, people talked about it the way they had never talked about other books."[2] Monteiro Lobato waxes even more bombastic: "*The Masters and the Slaves* erupted into our literary skies like Halley's comet."[3] Writers Gilberto Amado and Antônio Risério adopt psychoanalytical terms—*distabuzação* and *desrecalque*—to discuss the collective result of Freyre's work. And later, Antônio Cândido, commenting on Sérgio Buarque de Holanda's *Raízes do Brasil*, wrote of its "liberating impact."[4] And such enthusiasm was not unrepresentative. Most commentators on *The Masters and the Slaves* highlighted the book's rupture with previous thinking on Brazilian culture.

This rupture can be conceptualized as an inversion of values, reversing the negative position that the mestiço and racial mixing formerly occupied in Brazilian culture. Instead of a degenerative influence, the cause of great national woes, race mixing could now be interpreted as a positive cultural process around which Brazilians could invent a new identity. Cultural products like samba, Afro-Brazilian cuisine, and Luso-tropicalist hygienic techniques became the signs of that identity. In *Civilização e mestiçagem* (*Civilization and Race Mixing* [1951]), Thales de Azevedo comments that Freyre "set off an authentic methodological revolution in Brazilian social history and cultural anthropology." That revolution could be perceived in this "entirely new look at race mixing," which was now assessed as "a phenomenon of an entirely different, and, we could say, a higher sort, with a positive meaning and social nature."[5] Another, more recent, commentator on Brazilian national identity, Roberto da Matta, adopts a more distanced tone: "It was the work of Gilberto Freyre that first successfully articulated that version of Brazilian history that all Brazilians like (for clear reasons, and hidden ones, too) to tell themselves about themselves: that we are a mixed, a mestiço culture."[6]

It was as if Brazil had awaited the "revolution" unleashed by Freyre, as if "all Brazilians" eagerly took up his version of social history as a mirror. These descriptions emphasize the suddenness and revolutionary qualities of the phenomenon: an instantaneous success, a liberating impact, a dazzling explosion. The seemingly instantaneous, spontaneous, and unanimous adoption of a revolutionary idea does not happen every day, perhaps because nothing in the social ecology of ideas happens that way. Still, there apparently existed a generalized and widespread expectancy in the Brazilian intellectual world, a yearning for something like Freyre's warm appreciation of race mixing—as we have already glimpsed in the relationships between poor black musicians and elite intellectuals. This expectancy resulted in the dazzling intellectual success described by Amado and da Matta.

One recalls the French hygienics movement's reception of the publications of Pasteur, which were saluted as works of genius much before their results had been confirmed by other scientists.[7] There was a space that needed to be filled, and Pasteur's microbes filled it ideally, not so much as a matter of truth as of intellectual need. As Bruno Latour writes in The Pasteurization of France: "An idea, even an idea of genius, even an idea that is to save millions of people, never moves of its own accord. It requires a force to fetch it, seize upon it for its own motives, move it, and often transform it."[8] Nevertheless, it is common to read narratives of "great discoveries" or "methodological revolutions" in which ideas seem to emerge out of nowhere and exist in a vacuum, the thoughts of fantastic minds, floating in almost total isolation from the world. This will not do. It is necessary to analyze the social forces that move the ideas, along with the forces that "conceal" the forces that move the ideas. Such an analysis of Freyre's work is not the primary objective of this chapter, yet a few comments on the matter will help ohow how samba became transformed into a national music.

Gilberto Freyre himself contributed not a little to the "dazzlement" with which his ideas were received and to the interpretation of their success as a matter of personal, quasi-religious illumination. Many have cited the passage of his preface to the first edition of The Masters and the Slaves, where Freyre affirms that "nothing about Brazil interested me as much as the problem of miscegenation."[9] Freyre proceeds to describe the following scene, which he witnessed in the United States during his period of graduate studies at Columbia University: "Once, after three whole years of absence from Brazil, I saw a group of Brazilian sailors—mulatos and cafuzos[10]—coming ashore from a ship (I do not remember whether the 'São Paulo' or the 'Minas') into the soft snow of Brooklyn. They gave me the impression of being caricatures of men, and I recalled a phrase I had recently read in the account of a U.S. traveler to Brazil: 'the fearful mongrel aspect of most of the population.' "[11] How were Freyre's horror and scorn transformed into admiration and praise? His explanation seems magical: "It was the study of anthropology under the orientation of Professor Boas that revealed to me the true value of the black and the mulato." And Freyre specifies that the anthropology of Franz Boas taught him "the difference between race and culture."[12] So, according to the testimony of the preface of Freyre's influential volume, only outside his country did the young Brazilian intellectual learn to place a positive value on the race mixing that he later came to regard as the source of our true national culture. Ricardo Benzaquem de Araujo comments on the famous passage: "As one can see, the scene constructed by Gilberto is truly a conversion story: We have absolutely sinful beginnings, then, a neophyte and a master, the possibility of transformation through study, and finally, the acquisition of a new and superior form of truth."[13] The work of other Brazilian intellectuals plays quite a secondary role in Freyre's story of revelation and conversion, as though the ideas of The Masters and the Slaves and the new appreciation of mestiço culture had come "out of the blue."

But let us look more closely. A passage of Freyre's 1921 New York diary gives a different version of his Brooklyn vision:

> Recently I saw some sailors of the Brazilian navy walking around in the Brooklyn snow. They seemed tiny, frail, without the physical vigor of real sailors. An effect of race mixture? On the other hand, in the article that I asked him to write for El *estudiante* — the magazine for Latin American students that I edit along with a Chilean fellow, Oscar Gacitua — the scholar John Casper Branner praises the Brazilian mestiço, even when not very, or not at all, athletic in appearance.[14]

Earlier passages in the same diary[15] show that the twenty-one-year-old Freyre had already come to admire the ideas of Franz Boas when he penned this sentence, but here he does not mention any anthropological antidotes to his uneasy doubts about the results of race mixing. Rather, the scholar who comes to his aid, John Casper Branner, is a geologist who had traveled various times to Brazil and published studies on the geography of the Brazilian north and northeast.[16] Once again, however, it is the authority of foreign scholars that legitimates "praise of the Brazilian mestiço." Freyre later switched his reference to a different foreign authority in order to promote his ideas among Brazilian intellectuals. The preface to the first edition of The Masters and the Slaves, in which he names Boas as the source of his new attitude toward race mixing, signals Freyre's desire to identify himself as an anthropologist. In truth, many other factors — or "forces," in the words of Bruno Latour — contributed to this famous anthropological revelation.

Freyre's interest in Brazil's undeniably mestiço popular culture developed well before his trip to the United States and his encounter with the anthropology of Boas. It appears that he was searching, in his studies, for a way to justify academically something that he already felt: a personal respect for race mixing and an interest in popular culture that he shared with other Brazilian intellectuals of his generation. He was on the lookout for strong arguments against the racial pessimism that formally dominated so much Brazilian thought in the late nineteenth and early twentieth centuries.

The vigorous popular culture of the Brazilian tropics had attracted Gilberto Freyre at least since early adolescence. At the age
of fifteen, he confided to his diary the shock he felt at his emotional response to certain forms of popular northeastern music:
"I'm afraid I'm a bit sentimental. How else to explain that I cried
like a kid recently when hearing a popular song all by myself in the
silence of the night? A song in bad Portuguese, but sweetly nostalgic, describing the end of the Christmas holiday: 'Time to burn
our nativity scene. / See you next year, if we're still alive.' " [17] Freyre
would soon overcome the fear that something was wrong with appreciating such manifestations of popular artistry. In time, he became one of the most intransigent defenders of what he helped to
define as authentically Brazilian popular culture against its Europhile detractors. This attitude is already present in Freyre's private response (again, confided to his diary) to personal criticisms
published in Pernambuco shortly after his return from the United
States in 1923, calling him an "exotic" lover of things foreign: "The
truth is that I identify with the most Brazilian part of Brazil. I abhor
these supposed defenders of Brazil against a native son whom they
call denatured or deformed by too much contact with foreign uni-
versities. I think that even Rui Barbosa . . . is wrong, very wrong, in
his enormous lack of identification with the basic, essential Brazil,
the Brazil (and I do not say this demagogically) of the people." [18]
Had Freyre seen Barbosa listening, teary-eyed, to Catulo da Paixão
Cearense, or heard Barbosa's praise of the Turunas of Pernambuco,
to be quoted shortly, perhaps he would not have been so critical of
the famous statesman.

Meanwhile, one must keep in mind that Freyre's growing respect for, and militant valorization of, Brazilian popular culture
never implied a condemnation of cosmopolitanism or modernism.
Alongside praise of the "basic Brazil," his writings express a profound admiration for writers like James Joyce, Ezra Pound, and
Marcel Proust. When modernism arrived in Brazil, Freyre wanted
to see it "Brazilianized" at all cost, and he approved of artists that
sought somehow to identify with popular culture and "the Brazilian situation." The following passage from his 1924 diary provides
an example of his insistence in that regard: "Mário de Andrade . . .

does not turn his back on Brazil. He is very different from the 'totally universal' Graça Aranha. But Mário de Andrade is still imitative—with what is modern about him more copied from European modernism than inspired by the Brazilian situation. To be fair, though, he is now trying to learn about the Brazilian situation outside of São Paulo—even the situation of Amazônia. And Oswald de Andrade is probably more cathartic than Mário." [19] If this passage in Freyre's diary sounds like the nationalist condemnations later leveled at bossa nova or Brazilian rock music (also accused of being imitative rather than authentic), it is precisely because, by 1924, Freyre was in the process of defining Brazilian authenticity.

That definition was neither rigid nor uniform. At moments, what Freyre calls "authentically Brazilian" seems purely a matter of political provocation, and at others, an appeal to regional diversity that denies the notion of national homogeneity altogether. His much later essay, titled "The Complexity of Anthropology and the Complexity of Brazil as an Anthropological Problem," explicitly recognizes the absence of any sort of perfect unity corresponding to the names "Brazil" or "Brazilian," and it expresses concern that attempts to create total national unity would unduly sacrifice "the regional spontaneities that enrich, rather than detract from, the common culture." [20] In another article, Freyre juxtaposes the idea of Brazil as cultural continent to the notion of Brazil as cultural archipelago to assert the complementarity of these apparently contrasting visions: "the sense of being a continent, a defense against the excesses of insularity; the sense of being a group of islands, a defense against the excesses of the continent." Perhaps he reveals his own preference for the claims of the "islands" by specifying a bit further on that "the sense of a continent would impose on us a limit (although a healthy, useful one) while the island sense would mean, a bit paradoxically, universalism and an adventure virtually without limits." [21] Freyre again highlights the complementarity of the universal (and the modern) with the regional (and the traditional) in a preface to his *Regionalist Manifesto* (first published in 1926). In direct contrast to a narrowly introspective "caipirista" regionalism, his 1926 manifesto encouraged "painting, sculpture, architecture that would be progressive in form but regional in substance."[22] The *Regionalist Manifesto* defends the delights of Pernambucan cuisine and launches a salvo of ironic attacks against the fawning admiration of foreign imports that "Rio and São Paulo think so elegant and so modern." It impugns bottled drinks and favors coconut milk.

But the *Regionalist Manifesto* also polemically announces some of Freyre's most basic ideas. Black cooks (and black women generally), practitioners of Afro-Brazilian religions, folk healers, the makers of popular music—these are the new teachers, the new keepers of Brazilian cultural heritage. "He who goes to the people," wrote Freyre, "finds himself among masters and becomes an apprentice." In "the people" he located "the roots and the wellsprings of life."[23] Differently from the way he presented things in his preface to *The Masters and the Slaves* a few years later, Freyre here recognizes his Brazilian intellectual genealogy by asserting that the power of thinkers like Joaquim Nabuco, Sílvio Romero, José de Alencar, and Augusto dos Anjos originated in their contact with "the people." Despite these evident similarities with Romantic nationalism of the German variety, Freyre's vision departs significantly from it regarding the idea of national purity. In Brazil, writes Freyre, one cannot "romanticize" about the supposedly pure roots of a national culture. To the contrary, Brazil is essentially "combination, fusion, mixture."[24]

This idea of Brazil as basically a mixture provides a counterpoint for the radically antiforeign attitudes of other passages of the *Regionalist Manifesto*. But Freyre's antiforeign attitudes seem politically, rather than intellectually, driven. Seeing that the cultural debate would not be won necessarily by the most coherent and logical argument, Freyre adopted a rhetorical strategy of ridicule. Here we see the antipositivist strain that he had revealed in a diary entry at the age of twenty-one, declaring his preference for "St. Augustine over St. Thomas, Pascal over Descartes, Nietzsche over Kant himself, and now James and Bergson over Comte and Mill."[25] Régis de Beaulieu, who accompanied Freyre during the young Pernambucan's first experiences in Paris, described him as "deliberately hostile to systems of ideas."[26] Freyre resisted logical coherence even in matters of culinary taste:

Speaking of the delicacies of Zé Pedro, [Manuel] Bandeira is always criticizing me for preferring English-style beef or mutton, salmon, paté, caviar, or canned food. "What kind of regionalist is this?" he asks, quite proud of his logic. The truth is that I don't pretend to be logical, not in my regionalism nor in any of my other attitudes. Just after I returned to Brazil, local delicacies delighted my palate no end. Not any more. Now I really miss some French and English dishes, and every now and then I go back to them, whenever it is possible to find them in cans or preserves. The palate is like the heart that Pascal talked about. It has reasons unknown to reason.[27]

Here we have the portrait of a Brazilian intellectual who finds himself divided between the delights of "Western" cosmopolitanism and the demands of a politically correct (and also heartfelt) defense of what is tropical, popular, and Brazilian. Here reappear the apparently contradictory desires of Afonso Arinos, that "letter perpetually returning to sender." How to reconcile the contradictory desires, the two palates? Must they be reconciled at all? Not if one preference does not imply the rejection or condemnation of its opposite. Freyre defended the mestiço, or regional palate, so to speak, because it had lacked intellectual champions, not because he really thought it superior. Caviar was also good, but it had too many apologists already.

Freyre's cosmopolitanism and his love for popular culture both have clear limits in certain aristocratic assumptions. And these were not just early assumptions that he later shook off. As late as 1978, when writing an introduction for his book *Tempo de aprendiz* (*Apprentice Time*, his collected newspaper articles from 1918–1924), Freyre lamented the elitism occasionally evident in his first public writings and proudly called attention to their expressions of "extreme sympathy" for some aspects of popular culture. But even rereading these articles at a distance of half a century, Freyre failed to notice their expressions of extreme *antipathy* for other aspects of popular culture, such as jazz and Tom Mix movies. It appears that, according to Freyre's definition, the concept of *popular culture* ought not to include the manifestations of "industrialized" or mass culture emanating from the United States. The attitude was, of course, not only Freyre's. Innumerable folklorists and proponents of popular culture thought, and continue to think, the same way.

Regarding the jazz that was being created and popularized around him in New York during his stay there in the 1920s, Freyre displayed nothing like the interest that he directed to samba in Rio de Janeiro five years later. His written mention of jazz is, indeed, quite as jaundiced as Theodor Adorno's comments on jazz and on "industrial culture" in general.[28] Freyre informed readers of the *Diário de Pernambuco* in 1921, for example, that U.S. dances were "barbarous," and that "this jazz" and "this ragtime" were "horrid" stuff.[29] A couple of years later, he explained in the same newspaper that the jazz accompaniment of "modern" U.S. dancing produced "stupifying" effects, and he went on to report the results of an experiment in which jazz was played for animals at the New York zoo: "The monkeys did not limit themselves to the apathy or philosophical indifference shown by the storks. In the monkeys, jazz excited murderous fury . . . even, though of this I am not positive, suicide."[30]

These are unsettling words from an anthropology student who, by that time, had already spent more than two years at the elbow of Franz Boas. It is interesting to contemplate, too, that Freyre must have been a classmate at Columbia University of the writer Zora Neale Hurston, who was shortly to take part in the Harlem Renaissance alongside Langston Hughes, author of "Jazzonia." Not once, in his articles remitted from the United States for publication at home, did Freyre mention the origin of jazz among U.S. blacks. How could he not have known? Instead, the ironic, superior tone of these articles seems intended to show the Pernambucan audience the refined taste of their neophyte author, to qualify him as an intellectual commanding their respect in spite of his youth. Good music? That was Richard Strauss.

"The detritus that comes to us from the United States and Europe, we gulp right down!" wrote Freyre, here worrying about the influence of jazz in Brazil. But "in the presence of things worth assimilating, we remain cold as ice, like pathetic dogs without a sense of smell." His suggested antidote was the teaching of "aesthetic dances" in school. Always, however, his lamentations and exhortations preserved a nationalist tone: "We could adapt from our most primitive Indians and blacks certain dances that might one day tour the world as Brazilian triumphs."[31] And these attitudes were not mere vagaries of Freyre's student days. In *Sobrados e mocambos* (*The Mansions and the Shanties*, Freyre's second major work, published in 1936), he repeats almost the same ideas in proud reference to the steps of samba, "rounded into something more Bahian than African, danced by Carmen Miranda to the applause of sophisticated international audiences,"[32] allowing performers such as Miranda to "sublimate" and harness the brute "energies" of Brazilian blacks. The aesthetic elaboration of popular culture, thought Freyre, would produce unalloyed benefits for Brazil.

Perhaps Freyre felt such enthusiasm when hearing Donga and Pixinguinha because the Brazilian people were themselves already "rounding" its rhythms into the vehicle of international "triumphs," no longer purely African, purely "primitive." Jazz, too, constituted a cultural bridge between people of different races, but without inspiring a similar esteem in Freyre, possibly because he encountered jazz at a moment of explosive commercialization in the early 1920s. At any rate, Freyre's cosmopolitan sympathy for Brazil's version of urban popular culture did not extend to all the world's popular cultures, as the example of jazz clearly illustrates.

We have to be enormously careful when affirming that Gilberto Freyre preached union between blacks and whites, between the common people and the elite. Here nothing is as simple as the "now give your hands to one another"[33] of Afonso Arinos. Diego de Melo Menezes identifies a "coexistence of diverse and even contractory" notions in Freyre, as well as "a passion for complexity, complexity that he is unwilling to sacrifice to logical coherence."[34] That description would fit Freyre's social ideal of "Luso-tropicalism," which he proclaimed a superior form of civilization because of its penchant to mix and change. Ricardo Benzaquem de Araujo shows in detail that Freyre imagined race mixing as "a process in which the singular qualities of [the constituent races] did *not* dissolve," that, to the contrary, Luso-tropical race mixing was a delicate balance among antagonists, in which differences coexisted in intense interaction.[35]

Mestiços, thought Freyre, were better adapted to this intense interaction, more able to deal creatively with the heterogeneous exuberance of the tropical environment. He believed that a Brazilian aptitude for differentiation, for feeling "at home" with diversity, had origins that preceded colonization of the tropics, origins reaching back to the ethnic and cultural complexity of Portuguese historical experience at the gateway between Europe and Africa. Above all, Freyre regarded adaptability as the special Brazilian genius, the mark of our originality and uniqueness among nations. Indefinability, in other words, defined Brazil.

According to Freyre, there was always a danger—in any society—that the constituent elements might isolate themselves and cease to interact. Here his ideas approach those of Sílvio Romero, though without proposing the "whitening" process that Romero viewed as the result of interaction. In a 1923 newspaper article, Freyre worried about the dissemination of Jewish population in northeastern Brazil precisely because those new immigrants tended to keep themselves apart—the same issue that Romero had raised regarding German colonization in southern Brazil. To illustrate his point, Freyre makes uncharacteristic use of the U.S. term "melting pot" (in English), and he laments the formation of a separate ethnic identity within the national identity.[36] Seventeen years later, at the beginning of World War II, he inveighed against cultural and political congresses that discussed how "minorities made history." Freyre insinuated that those who denied the primacy of Brazilian national identity harbored pro-Nazi sympathies, and he cited the following passage as an example of "anti-Luso-Brazilian propaganda":

What does not exist is a Brazilian people. On that point, we all agree. What exists is a Brazilian state, within the boundaries of which live various sorts of people: Portuguese, Germans, Italians, Japanese, Indians, and Negroes, to name only a few. . . . We do not recognize Luso-Brazilian ethnicity as the exclusive national culture, and we refuse to accept it as the basis of Brazilian nationalism.[37]

Freyre recoiled in horror at these assertions, which he identified as emanating essentially from German colonies in southern Brazil and which, he believed, put at risk the process of racial and cultural mixing.

The Mansions and the Shanties chronicled the decline of the unfettered tropical miscegenation that he believed so basic to the formation of Brazilian society. For Freyre, the turning point was the 1808 arrival of the Portuguese royal family in Rio de Janiero. The establishment of the Portuguese court in Rio led to an opening of Brazilian ports to direct international trade, ending the isolation previously imposed by the Portuguese colonial system. Freyre argued that, over the course of the nineteenth century, light-skinned Brazilians became ever more concerned about how they appeared in the eyes of European contemporaries, and a sense of inferiority induced them to conceal their regional customs and African influences. Brazilian cultural elements such as the modinha, hammocks, local cuisine, and folk varieties of religious observance now went out of style, along with the "intelligent tolerance" of difference that Freyre regarded as a characteristic of "Luso-tropicalism" in colonial Brazil. A well-defined, cohesive aristocracy arose, and the numerous cultural bonds between masters and slaves loosened. The dwellings of poor people of color, formerly located not far from the big house, were moved gradually to more distant, frequently less healthy, sites around the margins of plantations. Humble dwellings and the big house now seemed worlds apart. The "re-Europeanization" of the Brazilian elite was, above all, a process of exclusion.[38]

Freyre called for a reintegration of these worlds apart, a return to racial and cultural mixing. Like a German romantic nationalist criticizing the "Frenchified" pretentions of the Prussian nobility, Freyre attacked the artificiality of the imported cultural veneer. The author appeared to detect some signs of African influences recovering their social importance by the end of the nineteenth century, but, as Ricardo Benzaquem de Araujo points out, Freyre "furnishes little sense of how the barriers of prejudice were *suddenly* breached."[39]

Here, again, is the historical mystery of samba. How did Afro-Brazilian traditions rather suddenly regain a central place in mainstream Brazilian culture after generations of proscription? To explain that transformation in *The Mansions and the Shanties*, Freyre emphasizes the role of urban people of mixed race. Perhaps it was a rare pang of modesty that led him to say nothing of his own contribution, and that of like-minded elite intellectuals, to the fashionable rehabilitation of everything from the music of Pixinguinha to traditional rice pudding desserts. Clearly, he was not unmindful of his place in this story. Indeed, his narrative of "re-Europeanization," and his description of a personal epiphany in New York, together helped him transform his intellectual project into a demonstration of heroic empathy. In Freyre's utopian vision, cultural empathy could transcend social distances and reunite the mansions and the shanties.

Freyre explains the importance of *empathy*—another word that he apparently introduced into Brazilian usage—in the preface that he wrote for Jorge de Lima's *Poemas negros* (1947). The preface excoriates the "enemies of the picturesque" who denied the poet's right to adopt a northeastern, Afro-Brazilian idiom because he had not "himself personally suffered because of African or slave origins." Freyre's refutation draws an international analogy: "As if art and literature did not depend on empathy, the empathy that led a Tolstoy to identify himself profoundly with the most oppressed people in Russia, although he was himself of the seigneurial class—a count, no less."[40] The argument had predictable consequences. "Fortunately, Brazil has no black poetry like that of the United States . . . always contracted into postures of attack or defense," he wrote. "Instead, Brazilian poetry has a zone colored by the influence of Africa, but already quite diluted in a Brazilian solvent."[41] Jorge de Lima's African motifs make some of his poems miniature precursors of Freyre's own writings, as in the following lines from "A minha América" (1927), addressed to the inhabitants of the United States: "In the mouth of South America / A rainbow of all the races / Sings a different scale from yours." The rainbow symbolizes not the blurring of differences but their close and felicitous association, the infinite variety of their possible combinations. Freyre called Portuguese colonization "a splendid adventure" in which the colonizers "dissolved themselves in the blood and culture of other peoples, to the point of almost seeming to vanish." [42] Never mind that "seeming dissolution" could be a strategy for the preservation of privilege. For Freyre, the samba became another chapter in the "splendid adventure" of Luso-tropicalism.

This being the case, it is truly odd that Gilberto Freyre, who believed music to be the chief expression of the Brazilian national spirit, wrote so little about music. In *The Masters and the Slaves*, the modinha figures in only one passage, and samba, in a single footnote — neither time referring to the creative potential of cultural and racial mixing. [43] *The Mansions and the Shanties* cites samba's corruption as a "plebeian dance" (later to be rescued by Carmen Miranda) and mentions, on several occasions, modinha's embarrassed withdrawal from fashionable settings during the middle of the nineteenth century, thanks to the re-Europeanization of the elite. [44] In his third major book, *Order and Progress* (1959), which deals with the republican period after 1889, Freyre gives more attention to music, but still nothing like the space he devotes to literature. Beyond that, there are elsewhere some praiseful comments for the Rio-based pan-Brazilianism of Heitor Villa-Lobos, and little more. Perhaps this is the characteristic that Freyre himself described generally for the people of Recife: "Lovers of economy and silence, we avoid music." Hence his relative silence concerning so crucial a matter as his discovery of samba?

We shall not repeat that oversight here, but before surrendering ourselves fully to the rhythm of samba, we must travel a last, twisting road of the sort that appears to take us temporarily away from our destination. The matter involves one of the cultural mediators who helped bring Freyre, Pixinguinha, and their respective circles of friends together for the Catete Street encounter of 1926. Let us now give serious attention to the earlier question of how a French modernist (like Blaise Cendrars) appears in our story introducing a member of the Carioca elite (like Prudente de Moraes Neto) to a legendary Carioca sambista (like Donga).

7 The Modern Samba

ilberto Freyre himself declared in a 1926 newspaper article that "the influence of Blaise Cendrars" was one of the two principle causes of "the movement for the valorization of things black" in Rio de Janeiro.[1] Somehow, a French poet, a representative of the Parisian avant-garde, had taught his elite friends of Rio de Janeiro a respect for "things black" and "things Brazilian." Freyre is not alone in emphasizing the role of Cendrars in that "discovery of Brazil" by its own modern artists. And the activities of Cendrars are often used to explain yet another mystery (along with the mystery of samba, the mystery of race mixing, and the other mysteries that populate this book) surrounding the definition of Brazilian national identity. I refer to the mystery of the two phases of Brazilian modernism as described by Eduardo Jardim de Moraes.

> The first phase, begun in 1917, is characterized by the polemic between modernism and retrospection. This is a phase of modernization, of catching up and absorbing the recent advances made by the European avant-garde, and it lasts until 1924. The second phase [begins] in that crucial year, when Brazilian modernism turns primarily to the question of elaborating a national culture.[2]

The mystery lies in the transition from one phase to another—an about-face well exemplified in Oswald de Andrade's landmark 1924 collection of poetry, the famous *Manifesto pau-brasil* (*Brazilwood Manifesto*). Why did Brazilian modernists abandon "pure" avant-garde internationalism and turn to inventing a new, specifically national, image of Brazil to suit their modern interests?

Cendrars's relevance to this matter is signaled by innumerable authors. Eduardo Jardim de Moraes believes that the recent interpretations of Aracy de Amaral, Benedito Nunes, and Antônio Cândido exaggerate the French poet's influence, but the modernists of the 1920s seem generally to have recognized it. The painter Tarsila do Amaral declared that the trip she made along with Cendrars, Mário and Oswald de Andrade, and others through the state of Minas Gerais marked, for all involved, "a veritable discovery of the *deep Brazil*." [3] Mário de Andrade referred to these travels as "excursions of discovery," and Oswald de Andrade, in a show of gratitude to his French colleague, dedicated the poems of his book *Brazilwood* "to Blaise Cendrars, on the occasion of the discovery of Brazil."

⌐ Our modernists presented this "discovery" as a sudden revelation, an illumination (once again induced by an outsider, as in the case of Freyre's epiphany under the supposed influence of Franz Boas) that depended little on any Brazilian artistic movement prior to modernism. Mário da Silva Brito, one of the most important historians of Brazilian modernism, went so far as to say categorically that "the modernists have no teachers in Brazil, either because they are dead or because, even when living, they might as well not exist." [4] The modernists envisioned their moment as inaugurating a new artistic project in Brazil and on Brazil. This version of the modernist story, the one that the modernists so liked to tell themselves about themselves, effaced any links that might otherwise have joined their new project to the nationalist initiatives of Graça Aranha, Lima Barreto, Afonso Arinos, Euclides da Cunha, and Sílvio Romero, not to mention their Romantic "Indianist" forerunners of the nineteenth century. Only through such a break would their modern art fulfill the condition — to constitute a radical rupture with the past and with tradition — that defined it as modern in their eyes. ⌐

But things did not happen exactly that way. Concern with "the discovery of Brazil" in fact far antedated the famous tour of Minas led by Blaise Cendrars. Certain "nationalist" habits, long since influenced by a taste for "things Brazilian," already formed part of the daily lives of São Paulo modernists. This everyday nationalism connected them to the majority of São Paulo's political and economic elite, with whom the avant-garde artists always maintained cordial relations (not to mention family ties) despite moments of tension.[5] The São Paulo elite's own "discovery of Brazil"—really the redefinition of a relationship that had always existed in one form or another—was well under way by the time that Cendrars visited the city in 1924.

A pivotal event in the transition was the 1919 production of the Afonso Arinos play *O contratador de diamantes* (*The Royal Diamond Contractor*) in the Municipal Theater of São Paulo. Nicolau Sevcenko calls the play a "catalyst for nativist ferment" in the early 1920s.[6] Why such importance attached to a simple theatrical event? To begin with, *The Royal Diamond Contractor* well exemplified the populist nationalism of Arinos (who had died three years earlier) and even included the representation of a *congada* (an Afro-Brazilian street pageant) danced to the beat of drums by "authentic" black people who had seldom (if ever) trod the boards of the high-toned Municipal Theater of São Paulo. The other players and sponsors amounted to something like "a *Who's Who* of the Paulista plutocratic elite," including the active participation of the current mayor (and future Brazilian president), Washington Luís.[7] The resounding success of *The Royal Diamond Contractor* set off a sort of nativist furor in Paulista high society, making what had been no more than an intellectual current into a widely influential social fashion. In addition, the play made Afonso Arinos "the intellectual hero of the new era."[8]

The "nativist" vogue now advanced on various fronts. For example, there were a number of highly successful "regionalist evenings," in which distinguished young ladies sang sertaneja (folk) music to guitar accompaniment and famous writers declaimed poetry with caipira (local color) tendencies. Sevcenko mentions several other manifestations of the new "national passion," in everything from food to cinema, and he describes an intense process of cultural refashioning, in which diverse worlds of experience and expression came together. "It is hard to say with precision," he writes, "to what degree these slippages, overlaps, and fusions . . . were deliberate, and to what degree they were imponderable contingencies of urbanization, technological transformation, and/or oscillations of the socioeconomic structure."[9] The fact is that the

São Paulo elite appear to have delighted in the new taste for "things Brazilian," and they conceived a new pride in inhabiting the country that produced such things.

The modernist artists of São Paulo could not avoid the contagion of this popular-national pride, years before their encounter with Blaise Cendrars. They seemed entirely primed and eager for the meeting, well able to satisfy their French friend's thirst for exotic difference. Even in his most "futurist" period, four years before the premiere of the The Royal Diamond Contractor, Oswald de Andrade could write an article promoting the idea of a distinctively Brazilian tradition of painting that took advantage of "our vast hinterland," offering "the most varied scenery, the most diverse hues of palate, the most expressive types of tragic and opulent life." [10] Also before the visit of Cendrars to Brazil, during Andrade's 1923 stay in Paris, the Brazilian ambassador invited him to lecture at the Sorbonne, where Andrade highlighted "the suggestive presence of African drums and black singing . . . as ethnic forces contributing to the creation of modernity." [11] During that same year, the painter Tarsila do Amaral was already serving Brazilian feijoada in her Paris apartment for her avant-garde artistic friends, among them, Blaise Cendrars.[12] Amaral, it is worth pointing out, was not a professed gastronomic regionalist like Gilberto Freyre, who always arranged for regular shipments of northeastern delicacies to the various locations of his residences abroad. Any Brazilian who has lived overseas (and knows the difficulty of finding the ingredients for feijoada outside Brazil) can appreciate Amaral's pioneering feat. Did she have it all brought from Brazil? And who cooked? Tarsila? Oswald? Did our modernists go abroad with Brazilian servants?

Brazilian friends went down to meet Blaise Cendrars when he arrived in the port of Rio de Janeiro and took him to experience more things Brazilian. They were Graça Aranha, Ronald de Carvalho, Américo Facó, Prudente de Moraes Neto, Guilherme de Almeida, Sérgio Buarque de Holanda, and Paulo da Silveira—the last of these, a journalist described by Cendrars as "the fiercest chronicler of Rio de Janeiro." Silveira, writes Cendrars, "immediately exposed me to Afro-Brazilian cooking by inviting everyone for lunch at a little place near the port." [13] Both the Parisian feijoada and the lunch near the port suggest that these elite Brazilians were already familiar with the sort of things that so interested Cendrars. Yet these same Brazilians would later affirm that the French poet caused them to discover Brazil. Like good anthropologists, we should take their words seriously and try to find out what they meant.

Like the theatrical assemblage of *The Royal Diamond Contractor*, the French poet Cendrars juxtaposed, crystallized, and emphasized certain disparate cultural developments that his Brazilian modernist friends regarded with unconscious familiarity. Something similar had happened when Gilberto Freyre encountered the ideas of Franz Boas on race mixing. In both cases, the catalyst came to stand in people's minds for a much longer process of gradual understanding. The modernist avant-garde of São Paulo therefore thanked Blaise Cendrars for discovering Brazil even though they were the tour guides. So far, so good. But what brought the French poet to Brazil in the first place? Blaise Cendrars was "one of the most central, most visible, most celebrated figures" in European artistic life during the 1920s.[14] His résumé included several enormously influential books, scripts for experimental films, and plots for ballets, as well as friendships and collaborations with other renowned French modernists of the day, such as Léger, Milhaud, and Cocteau, to name only a few. Why his intense interest in "things Brazilian"?

Blaise Cendrars had an interest in black culture that preceded (and possibly determined) his interest in Brazil. As the decade of the 1920s began, Paris as a whole witnessed what James Clifford calls "a period of growing *negróphilie*, a context that would see the irruption onto the European scene of [many] evocative black figures: the jazzman, the boxer (Al Brown), the *sauvage* Josephine Baker." This was also the period in which "Picasso, Léger, Apollinaire, and many others came to recognize the elemental 'magical' power of African sculptures."[15] Clifford, in accord with the dictates of anthropological postmodernity, criticizes the early-twentieth-century modernist approach to African culture as racist and sexist. He also compares the modernist discourse to that of many later anthropologists: "Both discourses assume a primitive world in need of preservation, redemption, and representation. The concrete, inventive existence of tribal culture and artists is suppressed in the process of either constituting 'authentic traditional' worlds or appreciating their products in the timeless category of 'art.' "[16] Jean Laude, in his carefully detailed study of French painting on the eve of World War I, detects "tribal" African influences on French art in the decade before the war, and states that "after 1919, African art entered progressively into the public domain and into commercial circuits, becoming an integral part of the aesthetic pantheon."[17]

Blaise Cendrars was one of the principal agents of this "black invasion" of French art, the editor of an *Antologia negra* (1921) that juxtaposed traditional African myths and legends with poems and stories by modern African writers. The book provided material for his ballet scenario *The Creation of the World* (1923) with stage sets and costumes by Fernand Léger. Cendrars later explained that he had intended to include Brazilian blacks in subsequent volumes of the anthology (which never appeared).[18] By the time of his 1924 visit to Brazil, Cendrars had an urgent desire for contact with black culture in its real-life contexts.

There are conflicting stories of how Cendrars met the famous sambista, Donga. One version puts their meeting in Paris, where Donga was on concert tour with his and Pixinguinha's landmark musical group, the Oito Batutas.[19] But the French poet himself propagated an entirely more dramatic version of the story, one in which their meeting occurs in Brazil. Cendrars described his solitary wanderings through the poor neighborhood on Favela hill where, he said, the mayor of Rio had warned him not to go at all. Seeing that Cendrars was determined to explore that dangerous neighborhood, the mayor had supposedly offered him a police escort. The mostly black neighborhood of Favela hill, explained Cendrars, was a "completely savage" place whose inhabitants rarely went down to the other parts of the city at all, except during carnival.[20] Eventually, the intrepid Frenchman found a less obtrusive guide for his slumming, a mulato who seemed to know everybody and every place in town and who eventually took him to the Cinema Poeira, "a select black club," where (in this version) Cendrars met Donga.[21] Here is Cendrars's description of Donga from an interview broadcast on French radio: "He was a black of pure race, the perfect Dahomeyan type, with a visage as round as a full moon, always good-humored and irresistibly funny. He had a genius, the genius of popular music. He was the author of hundreds and hundreds of sambas." [22]

Cendrars goes on to relate Donga's pleasure at finding that the two had a common acquaintance, the erudite French composer Darius Milhaud. According to the story, Donga sent Milhaud a message with Cendrars, saying that he hoped to compose a samba entitled "Cow in the Eiffel Tower" to repay a homage that Milhaud had rendered Brazilian popular music in his "Le boeuf sur le toit." Milhaud's piece, in turn, was a musical quotation of "Cow on the Roof," a piece by one of the Oito Batutas. Cendrars's quotation of Donga in this story—"Paris, a city where I have never been"—signals the care with which such anecdotal evidence must be handled. Donga had, in fact, spent six months in Paris with the Oito Batutas. [23]

Darius Milhaud appears here, along with Blaise Cendrars, as another international mediator in the story of samba's transformation into the Brazilian national music. Milhaud resided in Rio de Janeiro from 1914 to 1918, as the private secretary of the poet Paul Claudel, minister of the French legation there. That is how Milhaud met Heitor Villa-Lobos. The two hit it off, and Villa-Lobos introduced Milhaud to Brazilian music in general and the music of Rio in particular, taking him to witness rites of Afro-Brazilian religions, to hear choro string bands, and to revel at carnival. [24] Milhaud must have made a few discoveries of his own, too, when he first arrived in Rio on the eve of carnival. Here he describes his encounter with Brazilian popular music:

The rhythms of that popular music intrigued and fascinated me. In its syncopation, there was a subtle hiatus, an indolent breathing, that I found hard to capture. So I bought a lot of Brazilian tangos and maxixes and tried to play them with the syncopation that moves back and forth, from one hand to the other. My efforts paid off, and eventually I could express and analyze that "little nothing," so typically Brazilian. One of the best composers of that type of music, Nazaré, played piano in the lobby of a movie theater on Rio Branco Avenue. His way of playing—fluid, indefinable and poignant—also helped me to understand the Brazilian spirit.[25]

Here Milhaud establishes no hierarchy between "high" and popular culture. To the contrary, he speaks of popular music and musicians with respectful seriousness. He subjects popular compositions to careful technical analysis and finds that they have things to teach the most accomplished classical musician.

After returning to Paris, Milhaud composed various works with a Brazilian inspiration, among them the suite "Nostalgia for Brazil," the collection of short "Dances of Jacarémirim," and the one mentioned by Donga, "Cow on the Roof," a medley of many melodies popular during the 1910s, which became the score for a show by Jean Cocteau. "Le boeuf sur le toit" eventually became the name of another of Cocteau's creations, a cabaret that became "all the rage, and a principal center of Parisian cultural life."[26] As one can see, Brazilian popular culture flowed readily back and forth across the Atlantic in the 1910s and 1920s, undergoing surprising appropriations in France, providing typical examples of the process called transculturation, and generating redefinitions of identity on both sides of the Atlantic. Brazilian, no less than French, popular culture was being refashioned by the back-and-forth flow.

In Brazil, of course, the dynamic was different. The exoticism of Brazilian popular culture had been its most seductive aspect in French eyes, something to be savored. But, according to Benedito Nunes, the transculturative "anthropophagy" of Oswald de Andrade aimed to shatter "the exotic aura of native culture." In Andrade's *Brazilwood Manifesto*, the ideal was "to reconcile native culture with a renovated intellectual culture . . . in a sort of hybrid plot to ratify the ethnic miscegenation of the Brazilian people."[27] Here nothing would be pure. Everything would be mixed, perpetually the beginning of something different. That essential instability became the chimera of Brazilian modernists. There could be no possibility of rest in the land of the Other, so to speak, because the Other was among us, even in "our blood." Brazil is "a rich ethnic formation," wrote Oswald de Andrade, bringing us back, ever again, to the issue of race mixing in Brazilian identity.

The issue does not have an easy solution. Whoever intends to aid in the construction of Brazilian mestiço nationalism must define the mix in question, and the selection of one ethnic recipe as definitively "Brazilian" always implies the suppression of alternative possibilities. That is what happens in the writings on Brazilian music by another celebrated member of the Cendrars expedition to discover Brazil in 1924: Mário de Andrade. In spite of his opposition to xenophobia, exclusivism, unilateralism, and (principally) exoticism, Mário de Andrade supported the nationalization of Brazilian art and culture. He asserted the responsibility of each Brazilian to repudiate antinational manifestations—including those he considered to be of undeniable artistic merit—"even more than Russia does with Stravinsky and Kandinsky." [28]

This assertion (drawn from his *Essay on Brazilian Music*, 1928) seems particularly surprising from a modernist from São Paulo, because the regionalists of Pernambuco themselves might never have dared to make such a declaration. Also in 1928, Andrade published *Macunaíma*, that most nationalist novel by a Brazilian modernist, with its pointedly mestiço protagonist. Mário de Andrade knew that his nationalism was a political construction, a political choice for that particular moment in Brazilian history, and not the discovery of Brazilian roots or the immutable essence of the Brazilian people. His *Essay on Brazilian Music* inveighed against "puerile" exoticism, which he described as "the falsification of the Brazilian entity" by local modernists under the influence of "the opinion of a European." Mário's comment may have been directed at none other than his friend Blaise Cendrars. "In music, the Europeans who visit us insist on searching for what is spicy and unusual," he wrote. "If they hear the heavy drumming of a *batuque*, great, they love it. But if it is a *modinha* without syncopation, or certain lyrical effusions in the *tanguinhos* of Marcelo Tumpinambá, they make a face, saying That's Italian music." [29] He argued that European exoticism deprived Brazilian artists of their right to deal in elements of universal exposition, and he criticized extravagant musical gestures of a sort never before heard in erudite music as "not at all a natural and necessary expression of nationality."[30]

That line of argument could lead to a definition of Brazilian music to include all music created in Brazil "whether or not it has an ethnic character." But if a Brazilian composer "wrote [an opera] in German on a Chinese theme" with "so-called universal music," would the result really be Brazilian?[31] In theory, the answer was yes, but Mário believed that in practice Brazilians should resist such a composite as "antinational."

Here, without much explanation, Mário de Andrade's political concerns enter the picture. The moment in which he wrote—the late 1920s—called for "nationalization," he believed, and so Brazilian "composers should base their work on, or at least take inspiration in, folklore."[32] In a letter to Joaquim Inojosa, historian of the Pernambucan regionalist and modernist movement, Andrade wrote that Brazilian music should "reflect the musical characteristics of the race."[33] Where could those characteristics be found? In popular music, of course. And what was the true popular music of Brazil? Folk music, defined, at the time, in strictly rural terms. Thus, Andrade (like Freyre) distanced himself from what he called, in various places, "the deleterious influence of urbanism"[34] or "cheap vulgarity" or the "fatal internationalism of urban environments that softens national values."[35] He asserted all this, though recognizing the sometimes blurry boundaries between city and countryside and the existence of seductive urban musical styles such as that of Rio de Janeiro—whose guitar, flute, or saxophone players worked creative mischief on the standard repertoire, giving it a maxixe twist that could be danced with a dynamism "astonishing to behold."[36]

National music, by one definition or another, soon became de rigueur, and a sort of "national music patrol" enforced the order of the day. By the end of the 1920s, the nationalist about-face of Brazilian modernism had been consolidated, and the writer Antônio de Alcântara Machado already felt the need to protest mildly: "Today writing Brazilian-style has become systematized, compelled by fashion."[37] Did samba become a fashion, too?

8 Samba of My Native Land

The Brazilian revolutionaries of 1930 possessed an ideal new medium for preaching unification on a national scale: radio. The first radio broadcasts had taken place only a few years before, in 1922, during the centenary commemorations of Brazilian independence. The first station, the Radio Society of Rio de Janeiro, was inaugurated the following year. At first, its programming (conceived as "what the people need") consisted exclusively of classical music and educational lectures on "high" cultural topics.[1] Other stations quickly competed with the first one, however—commercial stations like Radio Mayrink Veiga, and Educational Radio, created in 1926 and 1927, respectively. Still, the radio did not acquire a mass audience until after the revolution of 1930. Getúlio Vargas, brought to power by that revolution, demonstrated a keen sense of how radio could contribute to his project of national unification. Later in his long rule, he proclaimed that even small towns should have public radio loudspeakers to keep the inhabitants informed of national issues, especially in the absence of nationally distributed newspapers.[2]

The first radio show to gain a truly wide appeal was the Casé Program, which began to broadcast popular music in 1932. Then National Radio followed suit, with transmissions of popular music on shortwave as well as normal commercial frequencies, reaching the far corners of Brazil and becoming the most influential broadcast medium of the Vargas years. Even the "Hour of Brazil," an official program of political outreach created during the Vargas dictatorship—and still a mandatory feature of Brazilian radio programming today—included popular music, so there could be little doubt of that music's importance in attracting a mass audience. The programs with the largest national audiences were all broadcast from Rio.[3]

Also growing at a revolutionary rhythm was the Brazilian record market, with the advent of new electrical recording techniques (replacing the older mechanical ones) and the installation of various recording studios. Until 1928, only one operation, Casa Edison, released local recordings for the Brazilian market, but three more labels were founded in that year—Parlophon, Odeon, and Columbia—followed the next year by Brunswick and RCA. All of these studios were located in Rio, and all of them needed musicians.

What could be more propitious for the city's popular music? In the 1930s, recording and broadcast technology came together with the political will to create a unified national culture, and this confluence occurred precisely in Rio de Janeiro (still, at this time, the national capital). Carioca samba, a set of local styles peculiar to Rio, was about to be crystallized and projected nationally as Brazilian samba. The urban music of Rio de Janeiro could not be imposed, exactly, in other Brazilian cities, whose inhabitants would adopt or reject it for their own reasons. But samba now "had it all"—or, at least, everything it needed—to become a national style.

At the beginning of the twentieth century, the popular music heard in Brazil encompassed an extreme variety of styles and rhythms, many of them not Brazilian at all. Carnival itself, described by Oswald de Andrade as "the religious event of the race," did not move exclusively to Brazilian music. To the contrary, the greatest hits of the season, reaching back to the first mid-nineteenth-century carnival balls (aristocratic as well as popular ones), were generally polkas, waltzes, mazurkas, schottisches, tangos, and later U.S. novelties like Charlestons and fox-trots. Carnival music originating in Brazil also varied greatly according to fluctuating fashions—maxixes, modas, marchas, cateretês, and *desafios sertanejos*—none of them coming close to contemporary samba's total domination of the festival, none of them considered to be a "national rhythm."

Only in the 1930s did Carioca samba "colonize" Brazilian carnival and become a national symbol. Thereafter, samba would be considered representative of the nation, while other Brazilian musical genres would be considered merely *regional* styles. Thus, in a 1976 interview, Lupiscínio Rodrigues, a sambista from the southern state of Rio Grande do Sul, distinguished his music from that of fellow Rio Grandense performer Teixeirinha (a cultivator of rural, "*gaúcho*" styles) in the following manner: "The difference is that I make popular music and Teixeirinha makes *regional* music." Asked why he had abandoned the regional influences of Rio Grande do Sul, Rodrigues replied: "I think Brazilian rhythm is the best in the world."[4] Suggestively, he felt no need to specify that "Brazilian rhythm," synonymous, in his mind, with "popular music," could only mean the samba of Rio de Janeiro.

The absence, before the 1930s, of a single Brazilian rhythm defined as such and exclusive of others did not indicate the absence of musical styles spanning various regions and social classes. The example of the modinha, examined in Chapter 3, shows how a particular style of music originating in Brazil could become fashionable in the whole country, and even abroad, without becoming *the* national music, exclusively definitive of what is most Brazilian in Brazil. This chapter will examine how Carioca samba attained that status.

Donga and Pixinguinha, the black sambistas who provided an evening of Rio local color for Gilberto Freyre and friends at their Catete Street encounter of 1926, had played all sorts of carnival music. In 1914, they helped form a carnival group called Caxangá, along with João Pernambuco, whose very name indicates affiliations reaching far beyond Rio de Janeiro and whom the reader may recall in connection with Catulo da Paixão Cearense. The Caxangá Group played at five successive carnivals, while, during the rest of the year, its members pursued other activities, many of them significant for the future of Brazilian popular music. Both Donga and Pixinguinha were friends of the famous Bahian woman Aunt Ciata, whose house on the square called Praça Onze became the scene of gatherings crucial to the crystallization of our national music.[5] "On the Telephone," the song that has gone down in history as the first samba, was composed collectively at a late-night samba session in Aunt Ciata's house. The later attribution of authorship to Donga alone gave rise to considerable bad blood among other members of the group.[6]

As described earlier, Rio de Janeiro was undergoing major urban reforms in the first decades of the twentieth century, reforms destined to eliminate the downtown housing occupied by poor families. These families included many black migrants from Bahia who had come to Rio after the abolition of slavery in 1888. Along with their other baggage, these migrants brought with them rites of Afro-Brazilian religions like candomblé and various musical rhythms that would soon be incorporated into Carioca samba. The northern part of the city became the main residence of such families, but downtown Rio retained, for some years, a multiclass character that facilitated the circulation of new styles through all levels of Carioca society. Our discussion of Afonso Arinos referred to visits that he made, in the company of other well-known writers, to a house in the old city center where Donga and Pixinguinha lived with other sambistas. These friends from different artistic worlds also went out together for an occasional night on the town. Many years later, Donga recalled the typical itinerary of one of these escapades:

> Olegário Mariano, Afonso Arinos (president of the Brazilian Academy of Letters), Hermes Fontes, Gutembergue Cruz, Catulo da Paixão Cearense and other poets dropped in sometimes. They went there to get us to go out with them. . . . We'd stay there playing, improvising, taking turns with solos, and the poets saying verses . . . and then we'd go out to that little square on Gomes Freire Avenue, Governors' Square, where João Pernambuco lived later. There was a bar on that square where we'd sit until daylight. It was a group of literary types who liked music and musicians who liked poetry.[7]

These recollections evoke an intense sort of personal exchange that constantly modified the cultural panorama of the city, renegotiating all its boundaries. The existence of such relationships could help poor musicians like Donga and Pixinguinha defend themselves against the sometimes hostile attitudes of the municipal authorities. Another pioneer sambista, Donga's old friend João da Bahiana, later recounted a colorful occurrence that reveals the workings of the kind of transcultural mediation so important to the formation of Carioca popular culture in general, and popular music in particular. The story illustrates both the repression and the protection the early sambistas received from the upper and middle classes.

João da Bahiana was the grandson of slaves who left Bahia after gaining their freedom and journeyed to Rio de Janeiro, where they sold Afro-Brazilian foodstuffs on the street. His mother, known as Aunt Prisciliana de Santo Amaro, kept several employees busy marketing her Bahian sweets. Aunt Prisciliana also competed with other Bahian "aunts" (like Aunt Ciata, or Aunt Amélia, Donga's mother) to see who could give the most animated parties, some of which became truly legendary and attracted people of all social classes. Prisciliana's husband was a freemason, and his masonic connections provided him with privileged relationships among the elite, including Senator Machado Pinheiro, one of the most powerful men in Brazil, and even Field Marshal Hermes da Fonseca, future president of the country, in whose battalion João later served as a coachman. Such luminaries might even appear occasionally, recalled João, at the parties given by his mother and the other Bahian "aunts." João da Bahiana played the tambourine, and once, in 1908, when he was playing it at the Penha street fair that many sambistas attended, the police confiscated it. "Samba was prohibited, tambourines were prohibited," explained João in an interview half a century later. Yet, shortly after the police took João's instrument, Senator Machado Pinheiro asked him to play at his house, and hearing of the lost tambourine, he bought a new one and had it inscribed: "For João da Bahiana, with admiration, Senator Machado Pinheiro." [8]

The story of the Oito Batutas illustrates the full web of cultural mediation involved in the national "discovery" of samba. The story begins with the worldwide epidemic of Spanish flu in 1919. At that time, the movie houses of Rio de Janeiro commonly hired popular musicians—including some important ones, like Ernesto Nazareth—to play in the lobby. Just before the carnival of 1919, the flu epidemic swept the city and created an opening for musicians at the Palais Theater. The manager of the theater, a man named Isaac

Frankel, had seen the Caxangá Group at a previous carnival and liked the music, but he needed a smaller band. Frankel spoke with Pixinguinha about his idea, and he and Donga selected six other members of Caxangá to join them for the Palais gig. Frankel gave the Oito Batutas their famous name (which means eight "batons," "pros," or "aces").[9]

The Oito Batutas made their debut still wearing the folkloric sertanejo costumes of the Caxangá Group.[10] They played flute, mandolin, tambourine, three guitars, *cavaquinho* (a small, four-stringed instrument), and percussion. Their repertoire included many sorts of Brazilian popular music, much of it Afro-Brazilian—maxixe, lundu, canção sertaneja, batuque, cateretê—but not "samba," which did not yet figure as a distinct musical genre, although all its constituent elements were represented somewhere in the other forms. In addition, most of the Oito Batutas were dark-skinned. By booking a band like that to play in one of downtown Rio's most elegant movie theaters, Isaac Frankel committed a daring act, and the negative reaction was immediate. The maestro Júlio Reis told the newspaper *A Rua* that the music of the Oito Batutas was "inappropriate for the educated ears of aristocratic moviegoers."[11] In 1922, journalist Benjamim Costallat remembered: "There was a real outcry when the Oito Batutas first appeared four years ago." And he went on: "According to those displeased, it was a disgrace for Brazil to have a black band playing on the main thoroughfare of its capital city."[12]

This journalist may have exaggerated about the extent of the resistance to the Oito Batutas. Discontent cannot have been that widespread in view of what happened next. A parade of distinguished personages—including Rui Barbosa, then Brazil's most revered political figure—attended the Palais Theater for the sole purpose of hearing the Oito Batutas play. Then, just one year after their debut, the band received a Brazilian government invitation to perform for the king and queen of Belgium during their visit to Brazil.[13] And what about the invitations the Batutas got to play at the General Motors Pavillion and the U.S. Embassy—the ambassador reportedly being a fan[14]—during the centennial commemoration of Brazilian independence? Not to mention the financing provided by Brazilian millionaire Arnaldo Guinle [15] for the Oito Batutas' tours, including their French tour, where they played for the former royal family of Brazil, now residing in France.[16]

Overall, it appears, unless the resistance evaporated over night, this black band playing "things Brazilian" had considerably more powerful friends than powerful enemies from the beginning. One thing is certain. Brazilian society as a whole was prepared to accept the Oito Batutas and their music, even to see them representing Brazil in official ceremonies directed at foreigners.

Basically, the Oito Batutas represented Brazil with rural folk music. As we have seen, their music was not homogeneous, but all the styles that composed their repertoire could, at the time, be called sertanejo music, which implied rusticity, even though some were really urban in origin. For example, a 1921 show done by the group in São Paulo was billed as "A Night in the Backlands." Catulo da Paixão Cearense was also referring to the group's supposedly sertanejo character when he complained that he would have been a better representative of that culture for the king and queen of Belgium to see: "If they wanted the king to see our backlanders and hear the songs of our people, why didn't they invite me?" [17] When Arnaldo Guinle financed a Brazilian tour for João Pernambuco and the Oito Batutas, the purpose was partly to facilitate their desire to collect folk music, then defined exclusively in rural terms. In other words, the connoisseurs of Brazilian popular culture tended to elide it, in these years, with the idea of a national folklore, and to identify that with the sertanejo phenomenon of northeastern Brazil. The Oito Batutas rode that wave of interest to national and international success.

Meanwhile, the offstage musical interests of the Oito Batutas were reaching far beyond anything that could be labeled "sertanejo," or even exclusively "Brazilian." During their 1922 stay in Paris, they became lovers of jazz, and Arnaldo Guinle bought Pixinguinha a saxophone. Toward the end of the 1920s, various members of the group played separately in "jazz bands" (with a varied repertory, despite the name) that were then being formed in Rio de Janeiro.[18] Donga and another of the Oito Batutas, for example, also played theatrical reviews with a band called Carlito Jazz, later touring Europe with it.[19]

This passion for jazz was reproached by journalists, who now initiated a type of nationalist musical criticism that became increasingly commonplace as the twentieth century advanced. The critic Cruz Cordeiro, writing in a magazine called *Phono Arte* in the late 1920s, reproved Pixinguinha for his obvious North American musical influences, finding fault, in that regard, even with the sambista's recently issued recording of the classic "Carinhoso." Foreign influence smacked of treason. "For this reason," wrote Cruz Cordeiro, "I judge that record the worst of the four that the Pixinguinha-Donga Orchestra have offered in the past two weeks."[20] The argument recalls the attitude of Sílvio Romero: Foreign influences meant imitation, and all imitation is necessarily bad. Later, the expression "North American influence" would be replaced by "Americanization," then "cultural imperialism," "neo-colonialism," and "the multinationalization of culture."

The accusations escalated along with the consolidation of samba as a quasi-official national music. That process of consolidation provided a standard of "authenticity" against which corrupting outside influences could be measured. Threats to this new standard could then be construed as undermining authentic Brazilian culture—something to be protected by definition and at all cost.

In a recent study of samba parading societies in Rio de Janeiro, Maria Laura Viveiros de Castro Cavalcanti shows how the parade designer (the *carnavalesco*) acts as a cultural mediator, negotiating among various social groups and various definitions of art and Brazilian identity.[21] Such mediations figure importantly in the history of Brazilian popular music, as we have already seen in the case of figures like Catulo da Paixão Cearense around the turn of the century; and the samba composers of the 1920s and 1930s exercised a similar function, connecting the elite and middle class to the world of popular street festivals like carnival. This mediating function was clearly indicated by contemporary observers, as in Manuel Bandeira's description of Sinhô, another frequenter of Aunt Ciata's house: "He was the most expressive link between poets, artists, and refined society, on the one hand, and the lowest classes of urban poor, on the other. That was the origin of the fascination that he awakened when brought into an elegant salon."[22] By the 1930s, the "fascination" of popular culture competed increasingly with the attractions of erudite, "high" culture in gatherings of the Brazilian elite. Manuel Bandeira, in a mood representative of general attitudes, could even present a Carioca sambista like Sinhô as the cultural symbol, par excellence, of Rio de Janeiro: "that which is most Carioca, most representative of the people, found in Sinhô its profoundest, most typical, and most genuine personification."[23]

At the beginning, the contact between this "genuine" Rio and its new elite connoisseurs occurred when well-recognized composers like Sinhô were invited into salons (or encountered in cafés, as in the 1926 meeting between Gilberto Freyre and Pixinguinha). Apparently, rich people with an itch to experience samba did not anymore, in the 1920s, make a habit of appearing at music parties in poor neighborhoods like Saúde or Cidade Nova, much less in the nascent favela of Mangueira, where most of the sambistas lived. Such neighborhoods exercised a certain fascination on the Carioca elite, but the "authentic" samba came from a territory they perceived as dangerous, too. "Everybody saw Sinhô as a sort of fabulous being who inhabited the nocturnal world of samba, a zone impossible to locate precisely," wrote Manuel Bandeira. He offered some vague coordinates and the assumption that macumba rites would not be far away from this "world where (one has the impression) people eat breeze, cure a cough with alcohol, and regard a little misfortune as beneath their notice."[24] And many of the well-heeled admirers of Sinhô—who so enthusiastically applauded his salon performances in the posh beachfront neighborhoods of the south zone—did not show up at his funeral, which occurred in his world, rather than theirs. Manuel Bandeira was one who did attend the wake, and he left the following description, which might be mistaken for a passage from a novel by Jorge Amado:

The little white chapel was too tiny to hold all those who loved Sinhô, all of them simple people: street toughs, soldiers, sailors, prostitutes (and those who kept rooms for their rendezvous), drivers, and macumba practitioners (like the old black, half-blind Oxum from Praça Onze). All the famous sambistas were there, and the black musicians who play *choros* in the little bars along Júlio do Carmo and Benedito Hipólito, also women from the favelas, Bahianas who sell food from wooden trays on the sidewalk, and venders of modinha sheet music. The flowers were in a little bar across the street—a sort of annex to the funeral chamber.[25]

In Rio de Janeiro, certain young men of the middle class were seeking closer contact with the mysterious world of samba. Mário Reis, for example, was in law school when he met Sinhô and began to take guitar lessons from him. Sinhô then invited Reis to sing on a 1928 samba recording, beginning the young man's career as a performer.[26] The next year, Reis sang on a number of recordings composed by another law student, Ari Barroso. Reis was the son of a successful merchant, and Barroso, of a district attorney.

Rather than being the property of a single ethnic group or social class, samba was beginning to function as a shared musical idiom, facilitating its ascension to the status of Brazil's national music. During the 1930s, other young men of the white middle class began to influence the world of samba. Particularly important was a group from the neighborhood of Vila Isabel, which included Braguinha (son of an industrialist), Noel Rosa (whose father was a business manager, and mother, a teacher), and Almirante (an orphan who worked as a cashier and served in the navy—hence his nickname, "Admiral").

All across Brazil, each new "regional" (as the bands specializing in popular music were suggestively called) inspired others, like falling dominoes. For example, when the Oito Batutas visited Recife in 1921, they triggered the creation of the Turunas Pernambucanos, who inspired the formation of the Turunas da Mauricéia, who, passing through Rio de Janeiro in 1927, called forth Flor do

Tempo—the middle-class group from Vila Isabel—all in a chain reaction, running from Rio to Recife and back.[27]

White middle-class musicians like those of Flor do Tempo lost little time in adopting the popular musical form born in the poorer neighborhoods of Rio de Janeiro. The radio commentator Haroldo Barbosa remarked that Vila Isabel in the late 1920s and early 1930s witnessed the same kind of bohemian artistic lifestyles as could be found among the middle class of Ipanema during the rise of bossa nova in the 1960s.[28] Flor do Tempo rehearsed in the house of a prosperous businessman, Eduardo Dale. Almirante (a member of the group) remembered Dale as "a man well connected at all social levels, who, seeing the little band as a good way to make contact with certain big shot politicos—influential types, useful for his business purposes—took [us] to play at the houses of ministers, bureaucrats, and directors of public offices."[29] By 1929, Flor do Tempo had become the "Band of Tangarás" and had begun to record sambas with a marked northeastern regionalist flavor: "When we left our Northern home / We left to show the world / How we sing up there." That same year, they produced the first samba recording with the heavy drumming—batucada—eventually standard for the parading "samba schools" of Rio's carnival.[30]

Noel Rosa's musical circle even participated in defining the "authentic" samba style. Rosa himself cowrote sambas with Ismael Silva, probably the chief founder of the premier samba school, Deixa Falar, usually regarded as the pioneer parade group of its kind. Rosa also did "fieldwork," according to his careful biographers João Máximo and Carlos Didier: "He always wanted to hear what those sambistas up in the favelas were doing, to trade ideas with them, to pool their experiences. Noel kept pounding the pavement in expeditions to Mangueira, Salgueiro, other hills, and to poor neighborhoods on the outskirts of the city—ears always open."[31]

Noel Rosa's pilgrimages took place in years when those favelas and poor neighborhoods were expanding enormously. The living areas of the rich and poor inhabitants of Rio de Janeiro were increasingly separated after 1930. José Ramos Tinhorão muses on

Noel Rosa's success in capturing popular taste in the 1920s, suggesting that the middle-class creators of bossa nova had much less success at that in the 1960s. He explains the contrast by reference to urban transformations: "Noel Rosa and his group lived at a time when the lower and middle classes of the city, although sufficiently separate to be quite distinct, nevertheless coexisted in the same urban area, so to speak, because of the proliferation of subdivided old houses and ramshackle tenements among the houses of 'good' families."[32] But simple proximity does not explain very much. Anthropological studies of life in big cities have demonstrated that diverse cultural phenomena can exist side by side without any interaction. Such interaction occurs when people—those whom I have called "cultural mediators"—move back and forth between groups, and this is not likely to happen without a propitious atmosphere or "field of possibilities," in Gilberto Velho's term. The field of possibilities operating in the popular culture of Rio de Janeiro allowed Noel Rosa to help define the popular taste of his day. Rosa's intervention occurred at a time when popular musical genres had not yet crystallized.[33] Bossa nova, on the other hand, appeared at a very different historical moment, when Brazilian popular music had already acquired well-defined genres with which the new style had to establish a dialogue.

The crystallization of genres in Carioca popular music occurred around the samba schools that paraded during carnival. Their music came to be known as *samba de morro*, referring to the hills (*morros*) where favelas were often located. By the 1930s, samba de morro had become the very symbol of Brazilian authenticity. The sambista and researcher Nei Lopes, one of the most vigorous defenders of the idea of samba's authenticity against "commercial" or even "imperialist" corruption, describes a genealogy of samba de morro reaching back to Angola and Congo.[34] On the other hand, it is interesting to observe how the supposedly "pure" and "authentic" article—later taken to embody strictly African roots—emerged from exceedingly "impure" origins. According to Lopes himself, the genealogy of samba de morro mixed various sorts of musical expressions, including maxixe (essentially a Brazilian way of playing and dancing the standard international dance repertory of the

1880s–1920s) before being purified by sambistas in the poor neighborhoods of north Rio. The sambista Ismael Silva, who took part in the final stages of that process, described it less as purification than as continuing innovation: "The [old] style of samba was no good for parading. I started to notice something. Samba went tan tantan tan tantan. No good for parading. How was a group going to get down the street that way? So we started to play sambas with another beat: bum bum paticumbumpruburumdum." [35] And this modification of samba became the "true" samba. At one point Ismael Silva argued with Donga, saying "On the Telephone" (which Donga claimed as his composition) was really maxixe rather than samba, and Donga suggested that Silva's composition "If You Swear" was really marcha rather than samba.

Who has the true samba? Where are its roots? Truth, roots—are these not the central mystery of any tradition? All traditions seem to require experts to pronounce on their purest and most authentic expressions. The freely innovating samba schools of Rio carnival soon acquired their own vigilant guardians of purity, quick to condemn any modification of the true samba. Paulinho da Viola set that attitude to music (samba, of course) in 1975: "Okay, okay, / I see what you say, / But don't change my samba so much. / The gang at my back is feeling the lack / Of pandeiro, tamborim, and cavaco [traditional samba instrumentation]." But how much is too much alteration? Who says what alterations are permissible? In a 1993 interview, Paulinho da Viola protested in more detail: "Before, everybody played in sync. Now, each percussionist does a solo. That compromises the true rhythm of samba and, the way I see it, impoverishes the whole thing." [36] But who defines "the true rhythm of samba"?

One thing is certain: The idea of preserving samba's authenticity and purity has considerable force. So much so that samba remains possibly the only genre of African American music—unlike Dominican merengue, Trinidadian calypso, Cuban son, and Martinican cadence—that has resisted the incorporation of electric instruments and other influences of North American rock and funk styles. This "preservationist instinct" has hovered around samba for a long time, since before the samba de morro was even invented, in fact. Jota Efegê cites an 1878 advertisement for a show that was to be held at Rio's "Skating-Rink," promising "true and reputable samba, that great Bahian dance, executed by four graceful women of Bahia."[37] Efegê muses that reference to a "true" samba must indicate the existence of a false, corrupt samba already in the 1870s. Possibly so, but the struggle for preservation of the authentic samba gained intensity when samba de morro became the official, government-sanctioned samba and when the samba schools became the center of Rio carnival in the 1930s. In 1929, the first parade of the pioneer group Deixa Falar was led by buglers on horses furnished by the military police.[38] Four years later, the parading samba schools got a subsidy from the mayor's office. By 1935, the parade of samba schools was featured on the official carnival program distributed by the city government. The newspaper O Globo sponsored the parade and formulated regulations for it, including "the prohibition of wind instruments and the requirement that each group have some women dressed as Bahianas."[39]

The nationalist regime of Getúlio Vargas was particularly firm in its official (and extra-official) support of samba and carnival. Less than two years after Vargas became president, as Rio's elegant Municipal Theater opened its doors to a carnival ball for the first time, the nationally appointed administrator of the Federal District (created to separate Rio, the capital city, from Rio state) assigned subventions to all sorts of parading groups. In a parade sponsored by the Jornal do Brasil the samba school Deixa Falar choreographically dramatized "Spring and the October Revolution"—referring to the 1930 Brazilian revolution that brought Vargas to power, not the Russian Bolshevik revolution.[40] A few years later, in 1937, the authoritarian national government of Vargas's New State decreed that the samba schools must dramatize historical, didactic, or patriotic themes.[41] The sambistas of Rio accepted the regulations, and the model of Rio carnival was then extended to the rest of Brazil, from Porto Alegre, in the far south, to Manaus, in heart of the Amazon basin.

Samba was fast becoming Brazil's quasi-official national music, even outside of carnival. In 1933, after a concert of the Orquestra Típica Brasileira (led by Pixinguinha), Vargas's minister Oswaldo

Aranha told journalists: "I can have only words of praise for what I have just seen and heard: people of my native land. I'm one of those who have always believed in our true national music. I don't believe in foreign influence on our melodies. We are a new people. And new peoples generally triumph over the older ones. Brazil, with its new music, its own music, is going to triumph."[42] Aranha's upbeat assessment synthesized various elements of contemporary Brazilian nationalism—its symbolic allegiance to the popular, its repudiation of foreign influence, its praise of Brazil's cultural newness and future greatness. In 1935, Heitor Villa-Lobos spiced one of his monumental presentations of "Orpheonic" song with strains of a samba by Arnani Silva, whom Villa-Lobos had met at a samba school rehearsal. In 1936, the national "Hour of Brazil" radio program featured music by the samba school Mangueira in a special presentation transmitted directly to Nazi Germany. One would like to have seen the faces of the ideologues of "Arian supremacy" (who, at the time, still hoped to establish a special relationship with the Brazilian government) as those Afro-Brazilian drums came pounding over the airwaves. The producers of "Hour of Brazil" seem not to have thought twice about the evening's program. Samba had already become the clearly established musical representation of Brazil in any international context.

Samba of Rio de Janeiro was now presented as a national "delicacy" to all illustrious foreign visitors. In 1929, the "sauvage" Josephine Baker got feijoada with samba at the Confeitaria Colombo, a fancy downtown restaurant.[43] Walt Disney was escorted to the see the samba schools in 1941 by sambista Paulo da Portela.[44] Jota Efegê likes to tell the picturesque story of the "famous Japanese painter" Tzuguharu Fujita who became so enthused with our "national rhythm" that he put together a samba band at the National School of Fine Arts.[45] It must have been the first encounter of Fine Arts students with samba, but it was not the last. The parade designs of artists with formal training have since strongly influenced the samba schools, as we have seen.

While these foreign visitors frolicked among sambistas, Getúlio Vargas invited the Banda da Lua—accompanists for Carmen Miranda—to play at receptions in the presidential palace. (His daughter Alzira Vargas had a friend in the band.) The 1939 New State National Exposition had a musical program organized by Villa-Lobos that featured performances by Carmen Miranda and sambistas Patrício Teixeira, Almirante, and Donga, as well as various (other) folklore presentations. The grand finale was a show put on by the city's chief samba schools.[46] In 1940, Villa-Lobos attended samba rehearsals sponsored in a favela called Quitungo by the New State's Department of Press and Propaganda.[47] In sum, the Vargas government's official interest in samba and "things Brazilian" was explicit and intense. From the Quitungo favela to the National Exposition, samba had become thoroughly "nationalized" by the time that the New State collapsed after World War II.

Within a few years, the samba of Rio de Janeiro had gained both official and popular recognition as the Brazilian national music, relegating other Brazilian musical traditions to "regional" status. In 1932, a number of popular musicians (one was Pixinguinha) combined with the famed maxixe dancer Duque to do shows with a rural, northeastern theme at what they called the "Caboclo House" (also called "the house of national song") on Rio's Tiradentes Square. Three years later these images of the rustic northeast were swept aside by a new theme: "The Kingdom of Samba."[48] The rise of samba was part of a larger nationalizing and modernizing project undertaken during the Vargas era. Brazil emerged from the New State with a National Steel Company, a National Petroleum Council, several national political parties (markedly absent before 1930), official praise for the national process of race mixture, and, not coincidentally, a national rhythm. In the realm of popular music, Brazil has been the Kingdom of Samba ever since.

9 Nowhere at All

The fifth of July, 1940, was a dark day in the life of Carmen Miranda. After her great success in the United States, after having sung at the White House for Franklin Roosevelt, she returned to do a show at the Urca Casino in Rio de Janeiro, then the most prestigious stage in Brazilian show business. She expected an enthusiastic reception, a repetition of the popular tribute that she had recently received when disembarking in Rio, upon her triumphal return from New York. But the audience's reaction to her show—which included new numbers in English—was significantly cool and disapproving, and Carmen fled to her dressing room in tears. A few months after the government's Department of Press and Propaganda had begun to sponsor its own samba parade group, Brazil's formerly acclaimed cultural ambassador faced the famous accusation of being a "false Bahiana." Canceling her return debut after its opening night, she immediately set about answering her vociferous elite critics.

She unveiled her answer—a samba called "They Said I Came Back Americanized"—a few weeks after the unhappy performance. The "Americanization" of Carmen Miranda, like the much-criticized foreign influence on Pixinguinha in the 1920s, caused a major flap, but such controversies eventually became routine. The issue of "Americanization" steadily gained salience in debates over Brazilian national identity as it took on centrality, too, in critiques of "cultural imperialism" or "cultural colonialism" all over the world. No Brazilian star would win a greater international reputation than Carmen Miranda—except perhaps João Gilberto and Antônio Carlos Jobim, the creators of bossa nova, whose "Brazilian-ness" was also called into question, as we shall see—and her international reputation had been constructed almost obsessively around her affirmations of Brazilian identity and representations of Brazilian culture.

Carmen Miranda was actually Portuguese by birth and never had a Brazilian passport, but she invented—with the help of other artists, like the composer Dorival Caymmi, who taught her Bahian choreography[1]—an image of Brazil that sold well outside the country. And that image, with its bananas and jangling bracelets, emerged at a time when the "mestiço paradigm" was fast becoming central to the consensual national version of Brazilian identity. Despite being white and European, Carmen saw no contradiction in dressing as a black Bahiana, the clothing later designated as the Brazilian "typical costume" to be worn by Miss Brazil in international competitions. Nor did she find it incongruous that her repertory concentrated on music and dance of Afro-Brazilian origin. These symbols expressed her personal allegiance to Brazil. They made her Brazilian: "Look at me," she said, "and see if I don't have Brazil in every curve of my body." No one in Brazil thought to criticize these pretensions at the beginning of her career in the 1920s, but with the gradual consolidation of samba as the Brazilian national music (symbolizing the mestiço as the quasi-official Brazilian racial type) people began to demand more symbolic coherence and authenticity from samba and sambistas.

Accusations of "Americanization" leveled at Carmen Miranda demonstrated the existence, in the Brazil of the 1940s, of a desire to police the use of the country's new national symbols. The mixture of samba with popular music coming from the United States, for example, had to be held within certain limits. A standard of authenticity had been established in the field of Brazilian popular culture. But who had the authority to distinguish what was "truly Brazilian" from that which had been "corrupted" by Americanization or any other international influence? This chapter will examine a few (and only a few, because there are enough to fill another book) of the debates that involved the defense of samba and other "really Brazilian" music against perceived de-nationalizing threats to "our true cultural values." The objective is to point out, as briefly as possible, some of the more recent effects of the valorization of "things Brazilian" that were raised to the status of national symbols by the triumph of the "mestiço paradigm" in the 1930s.

One effect that (in view of the cosmopolitan arguments of a

Gilberto Freyre or an Afonso Arinos) seems unintended by the early champions of "things Brazilian" was the crystallization of a set musical formula for samba. This formula, based principally on what is known as samba de morro, or favela samba, became a model to be preserved at all cost by musical nationalists. When bossa nova emerged to violate that formula in the late 1950s, many defenders of "true Brazilian-ness" attacked the new music as if it were high treason. While not necessarily a majority, the loudly articulated and widely circulated opinions of these critics constituted important public voices. José Ramos Tinhorão, well-known for his radicalism in defense of Brazilian musical authenticity, sums up their case against bossa nova: "After 1958, the so-called bossa-nova movement worsened the break with tradition [that had begun with samba-bolero and samba-canção in the 1940s], deepening the influence of bebop jazz while also modifying the traditional percussion of samba. Under way was a kind of schematization that seemed destined to convert this genre of Carioca popular music, especially in middle-class settings, into a kind of soft and amorphous acoustic pap."[2] Elsewhere, Tinhorão affirms that bossa nova was the creation of young upstarts who "broke decisively with the popular heritage of samba by changing the only original thing it had left, the rhythm itself."[3]

On the other side of that debate, bossa nova's defenders made different use of nationalist arguments. In the mid-1960s, Caetano Veloso wrote almost in direct response to Tinhorão. Veloso separated bossa nova from the egregiously Americanized productions of "performers like Johnny Alf or Dick Farney," whose compositions he regarded as beyond the pale, "an alienation of the underdeveloped middle class whose goal is to become like its counterpart in the dominant, developed country."[4] But Veloso saw no dangers of alienation in the creators of bossa nova, João Gilberto and Antônio Carlos Jobim: "João Gilberto really understands the mysterious idiosyncrasy of samba and is the best, among Brazilian musicians of all time, at playing with it."[5] In order to affirm this, Caetano had to qualify the notion of "traditional samba," recognizing its culturally constructed qualities:

If we admit the evolution of samba only to the point that pleases us, to the moment that we consider definitive, and then consider it crystallized, we might accept the *samba de roda* of Bahia and refuse to accept its earliest derivation in Rio de Janeiro, *partido alto*. Reacting against a loss of authenticity in samba, many have looked for the genuine article in the favelas and think that it only exists there. . . . But no one, in good faith, could accuse Ary Barroso of wrongful appropriation because he expresses himself in samba without having lived in a favela and without being semi-illiterate.[6]

Later, Caetano himself was accused of alienation and of betraying Brazilian music when he played his songs on an electric guitar at festivals in the late 1960s, initiating the tropicalist movement along with other musicians, like Gilberto Gil. In a 1967 interview for the magazine *Manchete*, Caetano waxed polemical: "Some people got hysterical when they heard the song 'Alegria, alegria' arranged with electric guitars. To those people, I have to say that I love electric guitars. Others insist that we should do folklore. . . . Now, I'm Bahian, but Bahia is not just folklore. And Salvador [the state capital] is a big city. It doesn't only have *acarajé* [an Afro-Brazilian dish characteristic of Bahia] but also lunch counters and hot dogs like all big cities."[7]

In 1968, Gilberto Gil described the people who reacted negatively to rock influences and to the use of electric guitars in tropicalista music as "young people associated with the movement of university students, who were conditioned ideologically to regard the music in a certain way, a group committed to tired social formulas."[8] Tropicalistas like Gilberto Gil struggled against those formulas. "We had to demystify that fascistic insistence on cultural isolation and on the national meaning of Brazilian-ness."[9] The poet Augusto de Campos defended the tropicalista project in a 1967 article: "A crisis of insecurity . . . [has] taken hold of Brazilian popular music, threatening to interrupt the march of its evolution —a crisis that has recently gotten worse, revealing itself in fear and resentment at the musical phenomenon of the Beatles, with their international influence and their local repercussion among young musicians."[10] The poet went on to compare the resistance against the tropicalista movement with that faced a bit earlier by the creators of bossa nova: "If these innovators had listened to the advice given then, by those who could only see bossa nova as the 'jazzification' of our music, about the dangers of using dissonance and so on, we would still today be exporting only 'macumba for tourists' as Oswald [de Andrade] would say. . . . Let's allow our music to move on. Unhobbled by prejudices [which he elsewhere calls 'supposedly nationalist']. Without partisan colors or identity cards."[11]

A similar appeal was set to music in 1985 by Gilberto Gil in his rock hit "Roque Santeiro." "Let him play rock," pleaded the song's lyrics from radios all over Brazil, going on to name a string of singers and bands that had become stars on the Brazilian music scene of the 1980s: Lobão, Paralamas, Ultraje a Rigor, and Titãs. Whom was Gil addressing here? Was there someone who did not want him to play rock music? The song was released in the year of the "Rock in Rio" festival, possibly the moment of rock music's greatest exposure to date in the Brazilian media; and the supposed "rock invasion" gave rise to a number of reactions in defense of "true Brazilian music." These nationalist defenders gathered allies on many fronts across the political spectrum. Dom Mauro Morelli, a Brazilian bishop, summed up many of the most often repeated nationalist arguments a couple of months after the festival, speaking here in the name of other Brazilian bishops of Rio de Janeiro: "We all agree that the rock festival brings with it two phenomena that make it inadvisable. From the social point of view—which, in my opinion, is the most important—it is alienating because it distracts young people's attention and energies from the grave problems currently affecting the country. . . . The other aspect is cultural. What does a totally imported affair like this—which clearly places little value on our own culture—contribute to Brazil's cultural horizons?"[12]

This kind of argument should not be taken for the isolated expression of a small minority. To the contrary, opponents of rock music can be found in various sectors of Brazilian society, and they voice their criticisms with frequency in the press. Although Brazilian musicians had been making rock music since the mid-1950s, with considerable commercial success in the 1960s, the term "Brazilian rock" gained currency only in 1982. This was a period of increasing popularity for Brazilian rock, marked initially by the hit "You Didn't Know How to Love Me," released on a CD by the group Blitz. The moment also called forth new diatribes by the cultural nationalists, who received more or less generous media space. They referred to Brazilian rock as "an artificial product,"[13] and "the expression of a people suffocated by international trusts," which, in the words of sambista Nei Lopes, "attempt to keep the great urban masses from consuming authentically Brazilian cultural forms."[14] On the other side of the debate were numerous defenders of Brazilian rock music (and, in truth, there were many sides, not just "for" and "against"). In a 1985 television interview, Gilbert Gil recognized that Brazilian rock descended, in part, from the earlier tropicalista movement: "You've got to remember that we opened a lot of space for these folks. The struggle over tropicalism plowed the field, so to speak, for [Brazilian rock]. Now we sit back and say, wow, look at what tropicalism did. . . . This is how we thought that things should be by 1985."[15] And, in the same interview, Gil went on to speak of Brazilian rock's supposed effects on Brazilian society decried by the nationalists: "You can say 'No, this is terrible. It will destroy Brazilian music, culture, economy, language, everything—the Brazilian soul, even. It is alienating.' It's true in a way. But at the same time that it destroys one kind of Brazilian culture, it is creating another kind."[16] José Ramos Tinhorão also discusses how tropicalism "plowed the field" for Brazilian rock, but with a rather different attitude regarding the results:

> Tropicalism . . . actually served as a kind of vanguard for the [military] government of 1964 in the area of popular music. The politically conscious middle-class university students attempted a defense of music of Brazilian origins, and once their resistance had been broken, the "universal sound" with its electric guitars could complete its takeover of the Brazilian market. So, beginning with the 1970s, instead of the musical exports promised by the tropicalists, with their stuff about "resuming a process of evolution," the rock era became firmly instituted in the media

and entertainment industries. In the 1980s, these satisfied—and colonized—spirits began, very "tropicalistically," to speak of "Brazilian rock." [17]

True enough, the vision of Brazil contained in the lyrics of 1980s Brazilian rock can hardly be called nationalist or patriotic. They present an unabashedly pessimistic picture. The band Legião Urbana, for example, offered the following appraisals: "In the favelas, in the senate, filth is everywhere" (from the song "What Country is This?" 1987). The Paralamas do Sucesso were hardly more encouraging: "Unemployed, cleaned out, without even a place to drop dead, indebted without a way to pay, this country, this country that someone called ours" ("Perplexed," 1989). And so on: "More fighting and burning, everything ends in a mess, the furious crowd set fire to the police cars, the prices run out of control, what madness in this nation" ("Disorder," by the Titãs, 1987); "We don't know how to choose a president, we can't take care of ourselves, we can't even brush our teeth, we borrow money and then can't pay, we are useless" ("Useless," by Ultraje a Rigor, 1985).

Irony, disdain, disenchantment, horror: there is no praise for Brazil, none at all, in these lyrics. Nothing like the samba themes that exalt the marvels of "the Brazilian race." "I'm all feet, I'm all earth . . . daughter of this piece of ground, I'm the Brazilian race," sings Elaine Machado in the title cut of *Brazilian Race*, a collection of songs by 1980s sambistas working against the rise of rock fever in Brazil. (The recording began the commercial success of the recent samba style called *pagode*.) Rock lyrics of the time present a Brazil more likely to create consternation and pity than patriotic pride. But they seldom suggest a superior observer, who is above all this, either. In the song "Brazil" (1988) the singer Cazuza communicates a clear sense of his own complicity in "the madness": "Great, insignificant country, I'll never betray you." And later: "Brazil, what's your business? Who's your partner? You can trust me." Other rock composers, in contrast, seem to divorce themselves entirely from emotional involvement in the nation. Some question the very idea that Brazil has a national identity. The Titãs's song "Nowhere at All" (1987) strikes the most radical attitude. "I'm not a Brazilian,

I'm not a foreigner, I'm from nowhere at all," they sing. And they go on to what many might think is the quintessential statement of the Brazilian rock musician: "I was not born of any nation." The statement in Portuguese—"Nenhuma pátria me pariu"—suggests wordplay with the expression "son of a bitch," substituting nation (pátria) for the word "bitch," or more precisely here, "whore."

It is interesting to compare these rock lyrics with the lyrics typical of other styles of popular music that emerged in Bahia during the 1980s, rising to national prominence—well exemplified in the career of Daniela Mercury—in the early 1990s. The music of the *trios eléctricos* (high-powered street bands that move through the streets during Bahia's carnival) and of the *blocos afros* (black parade groups who turn out for the same event) carved out a regional niche in the Brazilian music market, practically independent of the national music industry—with its recording studios and principal broadcast media based in Rio and São Paulo. Other regional niches had been similarly established in the 1970s by *forró* (the accordion music of the northeast) and *lambada* (of international fame, but focused in the far north of Brazil, around the city of Belém). The lyrics of the more recent Bahian styles clearly reflect their regional market. The music of the trios eléctricos is ebullient and optimistic, in contrast to the pessimism of Brazilian rock, and there are occasionally enthusiastic outbursts of nationalism in the Bahian music, as in the song "Brazilian Faith" (1987) by Chiclete com Banana: "Green and yellow [the colors of the national flag], I have Brazilian faith, I know what I want, I've got my nation." Yet, for the most part, the objects of musical exaltation in these lyrics are the state of Bahia and its capital city—as in the song by Gerônimo, "It Belongs to Oxum [an Afro-Brazilian deity]," which has been the informal anthem of recent Bahian carnivals: "This whole city glows," its "people radiate magic," and so on.

A separate chapter—or a separate book—could be written about the lyrics of blocos afros like Olodum, Muzenza, Ara Ketu, and Ilê Aiyê. Until recently, the blocos afros of Bahia used exclusively acoustic percussion and voices, in contrast to the trios eléctricos with their rock-style bands of electric guitar, bass, keyboards, and drum set. The blocos' musical arrangements (percussion and voices) correspond to their lyrics' thematic emphasis on black culture and African roots. These lyrics give a very different answer to the question of what it means to be Brazilian today. The question of Brazilian authenticity does not seem to be a thorny issue for a group calling itself Banda Reggae Olodum or Bloco Afro Olodum. The choice of words like "reggae" and "afro" reveal an embrace of cosmopolitan influences. This is a cosmopolitanism quite different from that of Brazilian rock, however. Like the rockers, the blocos afros turn away from nationalism to redefine their vision of the world, but they turn in a new direction: toward "the third world" and toward a cultivation of "negritude"—political and cultural solidarity with the African diaspora—not toward Europe and the United States.

Contrary to what one might at first think, these concepts are not used to exclude anything. The members of Olodum, for example, allow people of any race to parade with the group, and they freely mix musical elements of all sorts in their compositions. The third world and negritude are fluid concepts in the practice of Olodum, varying in meaning and importance according to the situation. In fact, Olodum is more open to differences—of ethnic, cultural, or whatever kind—than a typical rock band, and it insistently publicizes itself as racially the most democratic group on the planet.

Olodum is really much more than a musical or parading society. In addition to its carnival activities, Olodum puts on theatrical productions, runs a store (selling books, newspapers, and clothing with the Olodum logo), and organizes public debates and seminars on quite diverse topics. The group's headquarters are located in Pelourinho Square—the location of the whipping post where Bahian slaves were once punished. Over the years, this Pelourinho neighborhood had become extremely poor, in spite of being a national historical district and an obligatory stop on any outsider's tour of the Bahian capital, and the installation of Olodum's headquarters there led to a kind of community rebirth. Principally through its music, Olodum was able to instill a new pride and solidarity among residents of a neighborhood abandoned by the official policies of the city. So Olodum is really an integral part of a larger social movement composed of all the city's black organizations.

Nevertheless, Olodum is best known for its carnival performances as a "bloco afro," a term that gained currency in the late 1970s and early 1980s. The first bloco afro was Ilê Aiyê, formed in another of the Bahian capital's largely poor, black neighborhoods, Liberdade. According to Antônio Risério, the founders of this group emerged from the city's soul music dance culture.[18] Ilê Aiyê became famous throughout Brazil because of Gilberto Gil's 1977 hit song with that title, and lyrics saying: "White guy, if you knew / the value of being black / you'd take a bath in pitch / and become black, too." The frank formulation of issues of black pride and racial discrimination, so long submerged in official affirmations of Brazilian racial democracy, immediately awakened vigorous public debate. Most controversial was Ilê Aiyê's decision to let only blacks parade with their bloco at carnival time. Perhaps surprisingly for observers applying U.S. categories of racial identity, Ilê Aiyê's definition of black excluded people of mixed African and European heritage. Members of the white (and light brown) Bahian elite charged racism. But Ilê Aiyê was soon joined—with variations in approach—by various other blocos afros.

Olodum, the group that invented samba-reggae, is the most relevant to our investigation of Brazil's "national music." As we have already seen, the sambistas of Rio de Janeiro have, for several generations, considered themselves guardians of tradition, opposed to any substantial innovation in music of the genre. (The recent exponents of the samba variation called "suingue" have been the first to break ranks, in this regard.) The sambistas of the Bahian blocos afros, on the other hand, are not worried about purity and tradition. They freely create cosmopolitan mixes of samba and Afro-Caribbean rhythms.

Olodum's cosmopolitan inclinations are hard to perceive outside Brazil. The bloco's contribution to an album by Paul Simon (*Rhythm of the Saints*) was praised in the United States precisely for its "raw essence." Obvious reggae influences seemed to pass unnoticed. When one U.S. music critic did refer to "Caribbean strains

[that] remind you of hip-hop, calypso, merengue, etc.," he attributed the similarity to common historical roots, not recent influences.[19] Surely Olodum had not gotten some of its raw Brazilian essence from Bob Marley!

In my 1988 interview with him, João Jorge, the cultural director of Olodum, summed up their ideology as follows: "Olodum is very marginal," he said, "marginal in the sense of not having a lot of philosophical and musical baggage from the past. So we're postmodern, postpunk, postyuppie, posttropicalista." At another point in the interview, Jorge defined the music of Olodum in words that would have pleased Gilberto Freyre: "We're the synthesis. It's only possible to be Brazilian by being a synthesis of a wide range of colors, of peoples, of languages, of customs, of cultures. And music can only be Brazilian—new or old, current or traditional—by synthesizing and not excluding." [20] João Jorge's words may seem odd, coming, as they do, from a leading member of the Bahian movement for black consciousness and black solidarity. One would expect some sort of exclusion, particularly exclusion of the white elite, to be part of his cultural discourse. But it is not. Nor is Olodum set on preserving an "authentic" Brazilian or Bahian culture.

The transcultural rhythms of Olodum first won over the trios eléctricos that dominate the street reveling of Bahia carnival. In 1991, Olodum gained national fame and began performing in the most important venues of Brazil's major cities. The new Bahian music quickly surpassed Brazilian rock in the sales of their recordings and in general popularity, as the new sertanja (country) music had done a bit earlier. Commercial perspectives narrowed for start-up rock bands, which now depended on small nightclubs and independent recording studios—the "underground circuit," in the term that the rockers themselves like to use.

These new Brazilian rockers are quite different from their predecessors in the 1980s. A milestone in their development was the worldwide success of the band Sepultura from the state of Minas Gerais, who sing entirely in English in the genre called "trash metal" or "speed metal," and whose fame can fill entire stadiums in, for example, Indonesia. The Brazilian music magazine Bizz, in its survey of recordings issued by new artists between January 1992 and May 1993, counted 110 sung in English of 188 total.[21] This marked predominance of English-language lyrics in recordings is new in Brazilian popular music, even in Brazilian rock.

So Brazil does not seem to follow the pattern identified by the comparative research of ethnomusicologists Krister Malm and Roger Wallis in their book *The Music Industry in Small Countries*, which collected information on the recording industry and the penetration of "Western" music in twelve countries around the world. Malm and Wallis summarize some of their findings as follows:

> When the Swedish music movement exploded around 1970, thousands of groups suddenly started singing in their own language. The same process took place in Wales. . . . The first pop record sung in Sinhala was released in Sri Lanka in 1969. Through the 1970s Jamaica experienced the transition from rock steady to reggae. Kenya was producing the first Lou pop records. Other local tribal variants followed through the decade. The Tanzanian jazz bands were developing their own Swahili version of East African popular music. After almost ten years of copying the Beatles, Elvis, or Chubby Checker, musicians in the small nations started trying to develop their own national forms of popular music. Singing in one's own language or dialect was a significant change, since it introduced a new communicative element between performer and listener.[22]

Only after roughly a decade of international musical invasion (in the pattern described by Malm and Wallis) do local musicians begin to sing the new music in their own language and blend it with their own traditions. Then, another decade generally passes before the resulting, transculturated local music becomes fully accepted, "first by a youth audience, and then gradually by government authorities and national mass media."[23] Brazilian rock, on the other hand, was sung almost totally in Portuguese from the beginning. The rapid success of the first generation of Brazilian rockers (the Jovem Guarda, or Young Guard), owing much to their promotion on radio and television, shows that the country's broadcast media embraced Brazilian rock almost immediately, and certainly without a decade of lag time. And only in the 1990s did large numbers of Brazilian rock musicians begin to sing in English, inverting the progression suggested by comparative research.

A greater frequency of rock lyrics in English is only one of many new developments in Brazilian rock music. In the 1990s, all the important genres of Brazilian popular music have become notably more complex. Brazilian rock has spawned numerous stylistic subgenres (often with names in English: "metal," "industrial," "hardcore") that seem quite independent of each other. The mixture of international rock styles with various sorts of "traditional" Brazilian music is also increasingly common. For example, the Raimundos, a band from Brasília, blends "trash" and "hardcore" rock styles with the accordion-driven forró of northeastern Brazil, and many among their veritable legion of fans are the children of northeasterners who have migrated to Brasília in large numbers. Another example is Recife's Chico Science & Nação Zumbi, a band that mixes race and social classes (among the band members) and musical styles (metal, rap, maracatu, ciranda) in a kind of postmodern musical interpretation of Recife's famous native son, Gilberto Freyre. The idea of mixing international and traditional Recife styles to create "mangue beat," as it is now called, came originally from one of the whiter, more middle class members of the band whose poorer, blacker members came from a bloco afro that imitated Olodum's samba-reggae.

The creators of these new blended varieties of Brazilian rock evince little concern with "authenticity" or musical definitions of national identity. As Ana Maria Bahiana, veteran Brazilian rock critic, clearly saw already in 1986: "It is not really a matter of 'searching for roots,' nor a rockers' collective admission of 'mea culpa,' nor even a project of synthesis along earlier lines. To judge by what they say and play, and by what they imagine, we find ourselves at a new branch of an old road, a point where musical fatigue and boredom have been overcome in the search for new musical nourishment and ideas." [24]

There is no "nationalizing" project, no complex network of transcultural relationships at the base of these new musical fusions. This seems quite a different process from the one that transformed samba into Brazil's national music in the 1930s: a multitude of groups involved in cultural projects of their own, not devoted to creating unity of any kind. As Paulinho da Viola lamented, the community of samba is no more. But neither is there a rock community, or even a samba-reggae community. Does this also spell the end of the "mestiço paradigm," that version of Brazilian identity created with so much care and effort by many groups with a converging interest in "things Brazilian"? What can now assure the unity—even if it is only the musical unity—of Brazil?

10 Conclusions

In Rio's 1994 carnival, the theme presented by Mangueira—probably the samba school most respected by the advocates of "authenticity"—was a homage to the Bahian musicians Gilberto Gil, Caetano Veloso, Gal Costa, and Maria Bethânia. By an interesting coincidence, during that year's carnival in Bahia, Olodum selected a theme—tropicalismo—related to the work of those same musicians. Was Mangueira putting aside its devotion to the "purity" of traditional samba to invent a new Brazil, once again inspired in the Bahian example? Was it moving toward a more cosmopolitan blend, along the lines of the Bahian tropicalistas or even, in the self-description of the Olodum's cultural director, the new post-tropicalistas? No hasty judgments are in order here. In one of its several 1994 theme songs, the Bahian bloco afro sang "Olodum is hippie, Olodum is pop, Olodum is rock. Olodum has totally flipped." Mangueira, meanwhile, avoided the more polemical aspects of tropicalismo and its creators, presenting a "postcard" image of Bahian life. (I do not mean to be critical here. I am a postcard enthusiast.)

Although most Brazilians now prefer the music of Olodum to that of Rio's samba schools, the carnival of Rio de Janeiro remains the national festival par excellence. The elaborately staged parades in its Sambadrome are televised in full throughout Brazil, while Bahian carnival appears only in quick journalistic flashes of thronged streets. This is not merely an imposition of the Rio-based Globo Television Network. Even without the broad popularity that it commanded in earlier decades, the traditional samba of Rio de Janeiro continues to be an agent of national unification. Caetano Veloso himself said this in a recent interview: "Mangueira, and by extension, Rio de Janeiro, represent our national unity. Now that there's so much talk of separatism, it is good to strengthen Rio as a symbol of our nationality." [1]

Veloso did not say at all that the music of Rio was superior to that of Bahia, only that Rio and its music could better represent national unity than any other city (or any other music) in Brazil. His acceptance of Rio de Janeiro for that role was pragmatic and political. It did not signify a judgment that Rio came closer than other cities to embodying a Brazilian essence or the roots of our nationality. Brazil—its unity, our nationality—are constantly re-invented in a kind of daily plebiscite, and those reinventions should be carefully fortified to maintain a viable project of national unity. Only because many Brazilians still believe in that project—against regional segmentation, against a more "radical" heterogeneity—does Rio de Janeiro retain its validity as the emblem of that unity.

Beyond strictly pragmatic considerations, Caetano Veloso's ref-erence to cosmopolitan Rio (rather than to more Afro-Brazilian Bahia, or to Brasília, the capital city since 1960) also signals an affirmation of the ideal of unity through evolution toward homo-geneity, driven by racial and cultural mixing. Many still find in this Freyrean vision the special genius of Brazil, our own unique con-tribution to world civilization. In his poem "Americanos," Veloso presents an updated and nuanced version of some of Freyre's ideas, also reminiscent of Jorge de Lima's poem "A minha America" ("My America") of half a century ago. To people in the United States, writes Veloso: "white is white, black is black, and mulata, there's no such thing. Gay is gay, macho is macho, woman is woman, and money is money. That's how rights are bargained for, granted, won and lost up there. Down here, indefinition is the rule, and we dance with a grace that I myself can't explain."[2] Here, the "rule of indefinition" (between black and white, between man and woman, between the big house and the slave quarters) is still viewed as our principal characteristic, our great particularity, that which imparts our special "grace." It is no longer a matter of our being superior, as Freyre once suggested. It is simply our distinctive path to follow, a path inviable without national unity.

It all comes down to a struggle between contrasting ways of organizing, conceptualizing, or interacting emotionally with our national culture—or, according to Benedict Anderson's formula, contrasting styles of imagining our national community: on the one hand, the path of heterogeneity, where differences are clearly defined and encouraged; on the other, the path of homogeneity, where the rule of indefinition blurs or contaminates heterogeneity without erasing it. What consequences might a preferential option for this "indefinite homogeneity" have for our national culture?

The most obvious consequence of the homogenizing path—in spite of all the subtle qualifications that one finds in the Freyrean notion of it—is mistrust of any difference too strongly asserted. Hence, the most influential champion of African contributions to Brazilian culture rejected the idea of a specifically black Brazilian poetry. Freyre apparently regarded the cultural unity of nations as something extremely fragile, something only barely achieved by dint of great effort or because of a happy coincidence of factors unlikely to be repeated—something that a persistent challenge (like that presented by German immigrants in southern Brazil) might destroy forever. Freyre used anthropology to legitimate his role as guardian of Brazil's peculiar rule of indefinite homogeneity. It was not a failure to recognize the literary merits of pointedly Afro-Brazilian poetry that motivated his condemnation of it. Instead, he saw the issue as a choice of political priorities—like demanding Pernambucan cuisine to make a regionalist or nationalist statement, in spite of a secret taste for English roast beef. Freyre would have disapproved of recent attempts to rescue the "poetic alterity" of Africans and indigenous Brazilians by including purely Afro- or Indo-Brazilian texts in the national literary canon.[3] The path of indefinite homogeneity calls for any purely Afro- or Indo-Brazilian poetry to enter the national culture only as raw material for poetic miscegenation. Freyre saw the indefinite middle as always better, or at least more Brazilian, than the extremes. He applauded the practice of sunbathing, which became fashionable in the 1950s, precisely because it made excessively white skin darker, and therefore, more Brazilian. The type of Brazilian beauty that he lauded in his last writings was a woman of mixed ancestry, Sônia Braga, the quintessential mulata.

But how does one define a culture invented (or imagined, or projected) on the principle of indefinition? Is the desire to blur internal differences itself a desire to be different from other cultures?

Do other nations struggle with these questions? The matter directs our attention to basic assumptions about culture itself, assumptions that tend to become basic tenets of anthropological thought. Eduardo Viveiros de Castro describes one such set of anthropological assumptions:

> We think that all societies have a tendency to remain themselves, and, since culture is the reflexive form of their being, only violent, massive pressure can change or deform it. We believe that continuity is the very essence of social being, that memory and tradition are the marble marker upon which the cultural image is etched. We believe that once a society becomes something other than itself the earlier form is mortally wounded, that there is no going back to it, that lost traditions are lost forever, that the best that can be achieved afterward is an inauthentic simulacrum of memory. Only "ethnicity" and guilty consciences remain to dispute the space once occupied by the lost culture.[4]

Gilberto Freyre seems always to have worked against this anthropological credo. Everything that he saw in Brazilian culture, everything that he wanted it to be, pointed away from the permanence and immutability that characterize that definition of culture. Fluidity, the ability to change and adapt constantly, was the vital characteristic he praised in the Portuguese people and in Brazilian mestiços, alike. This sentiment finds an echo among many contemporary thinkers and artists, especially in Latin America. Mario Vargas Llosa, for example, has declared that "there are, always have been, and surely will be ever more intermingling" among Latin America's diverse cultural wellsprings.[5] Like Freyre, though for different reasons, Carlos Fuentes characterizes the mestiço cultures of Latin American as a sort of global cultural vanguard: "The whole world will become what we have long been, a world of [racial and cultural] mixing."[6]

There are contrary currents in contemporary thought, however, and many—perhaps an academic majority—view this perspective with deep suspicion. They signal the danger that a "mestiço project" would produce a world oppressively dominated by sameness. Contemporary societies have been engaged in an intellectual celebration of difference, what Jean Baudrillard has called "an orgy of political and psychological comprehension of the Other."[7] And mestiçagem always implies movement toward homogeneity that threatens to efface differences. Since the publication of Claude Levi-Strauss's classic essay *Race and History* several important international organizations have made it official policy to view cultural differences (and "differential distance") as necessary for the continued evolution of human society. Wrote Levi-Strauss: "All humanity lumped together in one way of life would be unthinkable because it would be petrified."[8]

The ideas of Levi-Strauss relate quite meaningfully to another currently influential notion: the law of entropy. Entropy can be defined as a measure of "contained disorder." But this containment is not favorable to the system. To the contrary (and somewhat paradoxically), when disorder is unleashed, it leads to a firmer integration of the system through creative internal interaction and equilibrium. Entropic heterogeneity (for example, the existence of two liquids with different temperatures in the same hydraulic system) becomes a precondition for the existence of complex, orderly interactions within the system. Without some heterogeneity, the system cannot create anything new. It becomes static and eventually "dies," at least until an outside stimulus causes a new internal differentiation, unleashing disorder and reenergizing the system by restoring some level of heterogeneity to it.[9]

Those who celebrate racial and cultural blending must address the dangers of entropy. In many of the passages cited in the course of this book, Gilberto Freyre suggests—as did Levi-Strauss— the value of maintaining an optimum, rather than a maximum, level of diversity. The problem lies in determining that optimum level. Freyre's vision of society is really anti-entropic, suggesting a permanent drift toward heterogeneity rather than the other way around. In the Freyrean world, it is producing social homogeneity that requires effort. Social homogeneity (instead of being the default condition of entropy) becomes a rare and fragile achievement, always vulnerable to the rebellion of heterogeneity. The second book of Freyre's major trilogy, *The Mansions and the Shanties*, can be seen as a description of one such "rebellion" in Brazilian history—the intense nineteenth-century vogue of imported European culture in elite society. His fear of heterogeneity's exclusive differences drives him toward homogeneity's exclusive uniformity, but he recognizes the danger. Precisely for this reason he celebrates the open, indefinite, and inclusive qualities of Brazilian mestiçagem.

Perhaps all this theory puts the cart before the horse. How does samba—and the complex process of its rise and maintenance as a national music—fit into the issues discussed here? A bit of recapitulation will be useful at this point.

First, contrary to the way that it is generally imagined, the invention of samba as a national music involved many different social groups. The favela dwellers and sambistas of Rio de Janeiro played a leading, but not an exclusive, role. Among those involved were blacks and whites (and, of course, mestiços), as well as a few gypsies—also a Frenchman here or there. Cariocas and Bahianos, intellectuals and politicians, erudite poets, classical composers, folklorists, millionaires, even a U.S. ambassador—all had something to do with the crystallization of the genre and its elevation to the rank of national symbol. Second, the crystallization of the genre and its symbolic elevation were concurrent—not consecutive—processes. There never existed a well-defined, "authentic" samba genre prior to its elaboration as a national music. Third, the whole process lacked coordinated direction. Even though some of the participants had much more status and power than others, they were not manipulating the others like helpless pawns to gain hidden, Machiavellian objectives. Instead, all those involved used each other for diverse, immediate purposes often having little to do with the overall "project." While some were interested in the construction of Brazilian national identity, others were merely trying to survive as professional musicians or to make a statement in the world of modern art. The pacts they made with each other were always provisional and renegotiable.

These affirmations should not be misconstrued to minimize the central contribution of black sambistas in the invention of our national music. Nor can we forget the powerful repression of black popular culture that undeniably influenced the development of samba. My intention is not to take away these important parts of the picture—already strongly emphasized in the existing literature—but rather to add nuance and complexity to them. Along with the sambistas themselves, many other social actors were involved. Along with the repression of black culture, other cross-class relations allowed the emergence of a definition of Brazilian nationality that turns on the concept of racial mixing.

In the early twentieth century, the great challenge for those interested in the cultural and political unity of Brazil was to select (or invent) national traits that the largest number of "patriots" would accept as exemplifying an essential Brazilian identity. The attempts by mid-nineteenth-century Romantics to use Tupi indigenous culture in this way had proved ephemeral. To abandon them and embrace mestiçagem as a defining national trait (while abandoning the older ideal of "whitening") was risky and original. Brazil was perhaps the first country in which mestiço pride and elements of urban popular culture combined to create a widely consensual national identity.

Viable national identities seem to require that the socially constructed national traits—inevitably products of complex negotiations—should be regarded by most people as things that have "always been so." Authenticity may be necessarily artificial from an analytical perspective, but the efficacy of such symbols as these depends on a sense that they are natural and authentic. No sooner had samba de morro been invented than it became the very emblem of a pure and ancient Brazilian essence, uncontaminated by outside influences. Preserving this musical essence (from changes in rhythm, mood, or instrumentation) became tantamount to preserving the Brazilian soul. The myth of the "discovery" of samba thus constitutes an integral part of the music's symbolism. The essence of the Brazilian soul, according to this myth, awaited discovery in the favelas, fully formed but ignored. For example: "In the old days," according to a representative memoir on the topic, published in 1933, samba was "repudiated, scorned, ridiculed." The vague but essential reference to "the old days" confers the historical depth required by the myth, but it refers in fact to a very recent past, the 1910s or 1920s. Then, in a sudden illumination, the country discovered samba, immediately recognizing its most profound cultural roots. As if overnight, in 1933: "Nobody wants to think or do anything else. Now samba is the study of literati, poets, playwrights, and even some immortals of the Academy of Letters!"[10]

The emergence of samba as the Brazilian national music exemplifies a kind of transcultural interaction common within complex societies. The coexistence of innumerable social groups with contrasting—and sometimes conflicting—lifestyles and worldviews requires constant, ongoing negotiation. Scholars as diverse as Georg Simmel, Alfred Schutz, Louis Wirth, Howard S. Becker, Gilberto Velho, and Peter Burke have researched similar processes in a wide range of complex societies. These processes can have very different implications, sometimes highlighting differences, sometimes commonalities: again, the path of heterogeneity versus the path of homogeneity.

This is not to say that the discourse of cultural homogeneity constitutes an ideological mask for a heterogeneous "social reality." I agree with Tzvetan Todorov that "discourses are themselves driving forces of history, not merely representations." Todorov continues: "Here we need to avoid the all-or-nothing alternative. Ideas do not make history on their own . . . but they are not purely passive effects, either. Ideas make acts possible, and then they make it possible for these acts to be accepted."[11]

In Brazil, the discourse of mestiço homogeneity, created through a long process of negotiation culminating in the 1930s, made possible and facilitated the acceptance of decisive acts such as the establishment of samba schools with state sponsorship. The result was a new approach to the matter of ethnic homogeneity, a new vision of the relationship between elite and popular culture. Despite their official nationalist endorsement, these innovations never became universal in Brazilian society. An outright repudiation of popular culture did not disappear from certain sectors of elite artistic taste. Racism continued (and continues) to exist. And an enormous and well-patrolled distance continued (and continues) to separate the elite from the poor majority. Nevertheless, substantial elements of the elite and middle class began sincerely to value Brazilian popular culture and abandon the ideology of white supremacy.

This multiplicity of "mental/cultural modes," this presence of contrasting social practices and contradictory discourses—together amounts to an inescapable characteristic of complex societies.[12] To further complicate this conceptual model, we should observe that complexity and unity can coexist and interact at many levels. Complex societies are always, in the multifaceted description of Edgar Morin, "at the same time acentric (full of spontaneous, anarchic interactions), polycentric (having several centers of control and organization), and centric (possessing one overall decision-making center)."[13] Given this suitably complex model for social interaction in complex societies, it is easy to see how movements toward homogeneity can coexist with movements toward heterogeneity. They are not necessarily opposing forces. Movements in one direction or the other will gain or lose momentum depending on a host of social, cultural, and political factors. To reduce all of this to a basic relationship of domination versus resistance, as social scientists have often done in studies of Brazilian society, is simply a convenient way of avoiding what Morin calls "the challenge of complexity."[14]

At this point, the full importance of who I have called transcultural mediators—like Afonso Arinos or Catulo da Paixão Cearense—can be appreciated. Let us assume that social heterogeneity generally comes first and that social homogeneity is primarily a symbolic construct. Transcultural mediation is required for this symbolic construct to become at all effective. How else will this be "a society" at all? Mediators of diverse kinds, with many different purposes, shuttle back and forth among social groups, putting them in contact with each other, constantly redefining the boundaries between them and remodeling the patterns of their collective life. The philosopher Gilles Deleuze (in a different context but with clear pertinence to the topic at hand) puts it this way: "Mediators are fundamental. Creation is about mediators. Without them, nothing happens. . . . It's a series: if you don't belong to a series, even a completely imaginary one, you are lost. I need my mediators to express myself, and they'd never express themselves without me: one is always working in a group, even when that doesn't appear to be the case."[15] Such mediation never has the capacity to erase social multiplicity altogether, even should that be the intention of the mediators, which it rarely is. Like the mythic trickster figure so common to the indigenous cultures of North America, mediators "retain something of the duality that they function to overcome." [16] Likewise, the Freyrean concept of the Brazilian mestiço retains, here and there, a trace of its constituent races (or cultures) despite being the center of a homogenizing project. [17]

However conceived or analyzed, the Freyrean project has had enormous and lasting repercussions in twentieth-century attempts to define Brazilian national identity. Is that because the path of homogeneity constitutes a "national preference" in Brazil? Not exactly. The path of homogeneity remains but one style in which Brazilians imagine their national community—when they imagine it at all, because many simply do not think of themselves in a national context. Still, the path of homogeneity has long been, as we have seen, the dominant one in Brazilian public discourse. Currently it seems to have gone somewhat out of style—to be working, at least, against the grain of recent history. Maybe there is no place, anymore, for the "community of samba" or for national communities imagined in a Freyrean mold.

In a peculiar and interesting way, the entire history of Brazilian national consciousness has been based on (and has derived energy from) the diagnosis of our "backwardness" in relation to the world's "civilized" countries. Many proposals have been made to "develop" Brazil, to make it more like the so-called first world. Gilberto Freyre—and all the others who promoted the idea of a Brazilian mestiço identity and facilitated the transformation of samba into a national symbol—proposed a different sort of modernity not modeled on the "first world," a modernity that incorporated the very cultural elements long considered the causes, or at least, the symptoms, of that backwardness. The nationalist project has now seen better days. Not only cultural nationalism, but economic nationalism, too, has been eclipsed in Brazil. The 1950s developmentalism of Brazilian president Juscelino Kubitschek offered its own emblem of a new national unity and modern identity: Brasília. But the new capital city, middle-aged at the close of the twentieth century, never became a widely recognized national symbol, and, despite the efforts of successive developmentalist governments, Brazil has not "won its place in the First World."

World capitalism itself clearly works against nationalist projects in late twentieth-century Brazil. We live in a society that has become globalized and fragmented to an extreme, creating a dilemma for Brazilians and other inhabitants of the world's "peripheral economies." "The failure of developmentalism," says Roberto Schwartz, "opens a specific, essentially modern period, the basic dynamic of which is disaggregation." This situation raises some portentous, and ominously familiar, questions: "And what if our portion of modernization is merely further dissociation, both within and without? Who are we in that process?" [18]

Today it is increasingly common in Brazil to hear declarations like that of Camila Pitanga (a television star) to a national news magazine: "They often call me *moreninha* [a euphemism meaning not-so-black]. They think they are pleasing me, but they're not. I'm proud of my roots." [19] This is certainly a victory against Brazil's own peculiar style of racism. But not so fast: To combat racism do we have to become North Americans like the ones in Caetano Veloso's poem? Must we put aside the ideals of mestiçagem and indefinition, forget about Jorge de Lima's "rainbow of all the races"? Does this mean that from now on it is settled, "white is white, and black is black"? Is that the only way not to be racist? Or is that just the easiest way to adjust ourselves, once again, to (fragmented) international capitalist modernity? Again, "who are we in that process?" Is there a chance, anymore, for a first-person-plural "we" in the story that Brazilians once so liked to tell themselves about themselves?

Once upon a time we discovered the pride of living in a mestiço country where everything is mixed together. Even the French sociologist Roger Bastide, who came to visit us decades ago, believed in that story:

> The sociologist who studies Brazil does not know what conceptual system to use. None of the notions taught in Europe and North America are valid here, where old and new mix together and historical epochs become entangled. . . . It would be neces-

sary to discover, in place of rigid concepts, ones that are somewhat liquid and able to describe phenomena characterized by fusion, ebullition, and interpenetration—notions modeled on a living reality in perpetual transformation. The sociologist who wants to understand Brazil must often become a poet.[20]

We were delighted to find ourselves so original. We might have continued to believe in our social poetry. We might have been the precursors of a postmodern hybrid chic, forerunners of a militancy that demands a multiracial category in the United States of the 1990s. We might have been what Roberto da Matta has suggested: missionaries of a synthesizing power that is rapidly evaporating in the world today.[21]

But we lost that faith. After years of criticism, we began to believe that the path of homogeneity leads in dangerous directions. A well-known samba says: "Whoever doesn't like samba can't be okay—wrong in the head or the feet, I say." These lyrics clearly represent the paradoxical flip side of the Freyrean project. Initially praised—and prized—for its openness to difference, the ideology of a mestiço Brazil eventually excluded diversity in the name of orthodoxy. That orthodoxy converted samba, the product of interaction among very different social groups, into an agent of internal "colonization." A national music born of indefinition came to define the rule, the only way of being authentically Brazilian.

Was that the original idea? Does it matter? Other ways of being Brazilian have always existed anyway. And they always will exist. They will always exist even if Brazil continues to be, forever, the Kingdom of Samba. Maybe, in some elusive way, the rule of indefinition will undermine its own orthodoxy. Maybe samba really is the best discovery—or invention, or mystery—yet produced by Brazilians.

NOTES

AUTHOR'S PREFACE

1. David Riesman, "Listening to Popular Music," in *On Record*, edited by Simon Frith and Andrew Goodwin (New York: Pantheon Books, 1990), 5.
2. This statement is from the principle manifesto issued by the CPC (Centro Popular de Cultura): Carlos Estevam Martins, "Anteprojeto do manifesto do CPC," *Arte em Revista* 1 (1979): 72–73.

CHAPTER ONE

1. Donga's real name was Ernesto Joaquim Maria dos Santos; Pixinguinha's, Alfredo da Rocha Viana Filho.
2. Freyre's book has been translated as *The Masters and the Slaves*, by Samuel Putnam (Berkeley: University of California Press, 1986).
3. Pedro Dantas, "Ato de presença," in *Gilberto Freyre: Sua ciência, sua filosofia, sua arte* (Rio de Janeiro: José Olympio, 1962), 197.
4. See the advertisement for "A epidemia do jazz," in *O Correio da manhã*, August 1926. Other movies advertised in the newspapers of the time included Charlie Chaplin's "Em busca do ouro," Eric von Stroheim's "A viúva alegre," and "De Santa Cruz," a Brazilian-made documentary on the indigenous people of Brazil that revealed a different facet of modernism, an interest in national authenticity. "De Santa Cruz" portrayed "the legitimate Brazilians," Indians of the remote backlands of Matto Grosso, who live like "strangers in their own land, outside of civilization, stoneage people living in the century of radium." The advertisement admonished its readers that "it is the duty of every Brazilian to know about Brazil."
5. Gilberto Freyre, *Tempo morto e outros tempos* (Rio de Janeiro: José Olympio, 1975), 183.
6. Gilberto Freyre, *Tempo de aprendiz*, 2 vols. (São Paulo and Brasília: Ibrasa/INL, 1979), 2:335.
7. Afonso Arinos de Melo Franco, *A alma do tempo*, vol. 1 (Rio de Janeiro: José Olympio, 1979), 65.
8. Dantas, "Ato de presença," 193–201.

9. Sérgio Buarque de Holanda, "Depois da Semana," in *Tentativas de mitologia* (São Paulo: Perspectiva, 1979), 277.

10. Gilberto Freyre, *Gilberto Freyre* (Rio de Janeiro: Agir, 1994), 75.

11. Dantas, "Ato de presença," 195.

12. *Correio da manhã*, 17 August 1926.

13. This samba was cited by Oswald de Andrade in his influential statement of Brazilian cultural nationalism, *Manifesto antropofágico*, first published in 1928 (*Obras completas* [Rio de Janeiro: Civilização Brasileira, 1978], 4:14: "We were never catechized. We lived through a somnambulist's right. We made Christ be born in Bahia. Or in Belem do Pará.")

14. Cited in Hermínio Belo de Carvalho, *O canto do pajé* (Rio de Janeiro: Espaço e Tempo, 1988), 94.

15. Gilberto Freyre, *Novo mundo nos trópicos* (São Paulo: Nacional/UPS, 1971), 330.

16. Freyre, *Tempo de aprendiz*, 2:329.

17. Ibid.

CHAPTER TWO

1. Antônio Cândido, "A revolução de 1930 e a cultura," in *Educação pela noite & outros ensaios* (São Paulo: Atica, 1989), 198.

2. Jota Efegê, *Figura e coisas da música popular brasileira*, 2 vols. (Rio de Janeiro: Funarte, 1980), 2:24.

3. Ibid., 1:122.

4. Peter Fry, "Feijoada e Soul Food," in *Para inglês ver* (São Paulo: Brasiliense, 1982), 51.

5. Ruben G. Oliven, "A antropologia e a cultura brasileira," *Caderno de Estudos UFRGS* 12 (1985): 12.

6. Gilberto Amado speaks of "distabuzação" ("dis-taboo-ization"). Gilberto Freyre, *Novo mundo nos trópicos* (São Paulo: Nacional/UPS, 1971), 124.

7. Fry, "Feijoada e Soul Food," 52.

8. Ibid., 52–53.

9. Roberto da Matta, "Digressão: A fábula das três Raças, ou o problema do racismo à brasileira," in *Relativizando: Uma introdução à antropologia social* (Petrópolis: Vozes, 1981), 83.

10. Thomas Skidmore, "EUA Bi-Racial vs Brasil Multiracial: O contraste ainda é válido?" *Novos Estudos CEBRAP* 34 (November 1992): 61.

11. Ibid.

12. Mário de Andrade, *Aspectos da música brasileira* (São Paulo: Martins, 1965), 31.

13. Gilberto Freyre, *Ordem e progresso*, 3rd Ed. (Rio De Janeiro: José Olympio, 1974), 104.

14. See Eric Hobsbawn, *Nations and Nationalism since 1780: Programme, Myth, Reality* (Cambridge: Cambridge University Press, 1990), and Richard Peterson, "La fabrication de l'autenticité: La country music," *Actes de la Recherche* 93 (January 1992): 3–19.

15. Peterson, "Fabrication de l'autenticité," 4.

16. Néstor García Canclini, *Culturas híbridas* (Buenos Aires: Sudamericana, 1992), 205.

CHAPTER THREE

1. Cited in Wanderlay Pinho, *Salões e damas do segundo reinado*, 3rd ed. (São Paulo: Livraria Martins, 1959), 27.

2. From L. F. de Tollenare, *Notas dominicais tomadas durante uma viagem em Portugal e no Brasil em 1816, 1817, e 1818*, cited in ibid., 29.

3. Gilberto Freyre, *Sobrados e mocambos*, 4th ed. (Rio de Janeiro: José Olympio, 1968), esp. ch. 1.

4. See José Ramos Tinhorão, *Pequena história da música popular* (São Paulo: Art, 1986), 1986.

5. See the entry for "modinha" in the *Enciclopédia de música brasileira* (São Paulo: Art Editora, 1977).

6. Tinhorão, *Pequena história*, 19.

7. The modinhas harmonized by Neukomm and published in Paris in 1824 were by Joaquim Manuel, another Brazilian composer of mixed race, according to Gilberto Freyre, *Ordem e progresso*, 3rd ed. (Rio de Janeiro: José Olympio, 1974), 104. On Neukomm, see "modinha" in the *Enciclopédia de música brasileira*.

8. Carlos Maul, *Catulo* (Rio de Janeiro: Livraria São José, n.d.), 65.

9. In addition to Cunha Barbosa, Maul specifically mentions Ledo Gonçalves (deputy-general and enemy of the powerful "founding father," José Bonifácio) and José Clemente Pereira (variously minister of empire, minister of war, and senator with lifetime tenure). See Maul, *Catulo*, 49.

10. Freyre, *Ordem e progresso*, 107.

11. Tinhorão, *Pequena história*, 20.

12. Ibid., 21.

13. Eunice Gondim, *Vida e obra de Paula Brito* (Rio de Janeiro: Livraria Brasiliana, 1965), 59.

14. Ibid., 59.

15. Mello de Moraes Filho, *Factos e memórias* (Rio de Janeiro: H. Garnier, 1904), 154.

16. Gilberto Velho, "Projeto, emoção e orientação em sociedades complexas," in *Individualismo e cultura* (Rio de Janeiro: Zahar, 1981), 16.
17. Ibid., 17.
18. Ibid., 32.
19. Michel Vovelle, in *Ideologias e mentalidades* (São Paulo: Brasiliense, 1978), uses the term cultural mediators especially for individuals who mediate between the erudite and the popular.
20. Mello de Moraes Filho, *Artistas de meu tempo* (Rio de Janeiro: H. Garnier, 1905), 145.
21. Ibid., 170–71.
22. Moraes Filho, *Factos e memórias*, 155. His fellow troubador, Catulo da Paixão Cearense, remembered him as a *preto magrinho* (Maul, *Catulo*, 40).
23. Moraes Filho, *Factos e memórias*, 156.
24. Freyre, *Ordem e progresso*, 104; Maul, *Catulo*, 41.
25. Jeffrey Needell, *Belle époque tropical* (São Paulo: Companhia das Letras, 1993), 77.
26. Mônica Velloso, *As tradições populares na belle époque carioca* (Rio de Janeiro: Funarte, 1988), 8–9, 17.
27. I don't know whether it is worthwhile to invoke the notion of "resistance" here, but Wilson Martins correctly criticizes Jeffrey Needell for overestimating the extent and depth of French imitation. See Wilson Martins, "Idealizações mentais," in *Jornal do Brasil*, Caderno Idéias (1994): 4.
28. The pageants in question are "*reisados*" and "*pastorinhas*" (Maul, *Catulo*, 25).
29. Vasco Mariz, *Heitor Villa-Lobos* (Belo Horizonte: Itaitiaia, 1989), 26.
30. Tinhorão, *Pequena história*, 35.
31. The description was published in *Correio da manhã* by the historian, politician, and journalist Rocha Pombo, cited in Maul, *Catulo*, 27.
32. Maul, *Catulo*, 27.
33. Cited in Jota Efegê, *Figura e coisas da música popular brasileira*, 2 vols. (Rio de Janeiro: Funarte, 1980), 2:128.
34. The interview was with the carnival memorialist "Vagalume," cited in Sérgio Cabral, *As escolas de samba* (Rio de Janeiro: Fontana, 1974), 15.
35. Lima Barreto, *Triste fim de Policarpo Quaresma* (Rio de Janeiro: Ediouro, n.d.), 16.
36. Ibid., 12.
37. Ibid., 16.
38. The chronicler was Luís Edmundo, in *O Rio de Janeiro de meu tempo*, cited in Tinhorão, *Pequena história*, 34. Catulo's big sertanejo hits, cowritten

with the guitarist João Pernambuco, were "Cabocla di Caxangá" (1912) and "Luar do sertão" (1913).

39. In 1900, the biggest successes were "O galo preto," a polka by Artur Canongia; "As priminhas de Marocas," a polka-habanera by J. S. Avellor, "O senhor padre vigário," a polka-lundu by José Soares Barbosa; and "Se eu pedir você me da?," a polka-chula by Avellor (Edigar de Alencar, "O Carnaval do Rio em 1900 e na Década seguinte," in Brasil, 1900–1910 (Rio de Janeiro: Biblioteca Nacional, 1980), 144).

40. Tinhorão, Pequena história, 86.

41. Ibid., 51.

42. Ibid., 58.

43. Ibid., 71.

44. The Grupo do Caxangá was a forerunner of Donga and Pixinguinha's more famous group, Oito Batutas, that began its conquest of Rio de Janeiro by performing in the lobby of the Palais Cinema, in the Cinelândia district, center of the city's fashionable nightlife in the late 1910s.

45. Quoted in Maul, Catulo, 44.

46. Cited in Sérgio Cabral, Pixinguinha: Vida e obra (Rio de Janeiro: Funarte, 1978), 27–28.

47. See Tristão de Athayde, Affonso Arinos (Rio de Janeiro: Anuápio do Brasil, 1922); Afonso Oliveira Mello, Afonso Arinos e o sertão (Rio de Janeiro: Borsoi, 1961); and the introduction by his nephew Afonso Arinos de Melo Franco, "O Sertanejo Afonso Arinos," in Obra completa (Rio de Janeiro: Conselho Federal de Cultura, 1969), 885–95.

48. Ronald Carvalho, "Ronald de Carvalho," in Afrânio Coutinho, Caminhos do pensamento crítico (Rio de Janeiro: Pallas/MEC, 1972), 733.

49. Nicolau Sevcenko, Orfeu extático na metrópole (São Paulo: Companhia das Letras, 1992), 239.

50. Athayde, Affonso Arinos, 44–46.

51. Ibid., 49.

52. Ibid., 30–31, 35.

53. Gilberto Freyre, Tempo de aprendiz, 2 vols. (São Paulo and Brasília: Ibrasa/INL, 1979), 2:79.

CHAPTER FOUR

1. Afonso Arinos, "A unidade da pátria," in Obra completa (Rio de Janeiro: Conselho Federal de Cultura, 1969), 887.

2. Ibid., 891.

3. Ibid., 891–92.

4. Ibid., 889.

5. Ernest Gellner, *Nations and Nationalism* (Ithaca: Cornell University Press, 1983), 48–49.

6. Eric Hobsbawn, *Nations and Nationalism since 1780: Programme, Myth, Reality* (Cambridge: Cambridge University Press, 1990), 19.

7. Benedict Anderson, *Nação e consciência nacional* (São Paulo: Ática, 1989), 14.

8. Ibid., 15.

9. Immanuel Wallerstein, *Geopolitics and Geoculture* (Cambridge: Cambridge University Press, 1991), 185.

10. In that respect, they are the intellectual heirs of the French thinker Ernest Renan, whose famous formula "A nation is a daily plebiscite" — in answer to his title question *Qu'est-ce que c'est une nation?* (1882) — could serve as the epigraph for this book.

11. Anderson, *Nação e consciência*, 29.

12. Georg Simmel, "The Nobility," in *On Individuality and Social Forms* (Chicago: The University of Chicago Press, 1971), 205.

13. Ibid., 204.

14. Hobsbawm, *Nations*, 69.

15. John Tomlinson, *Cultural Imperialism* (Baltimore: Johns Hopkins University Press, 1991), 92.

16. See Norbert Elias, *The Civilizing Process* (New York: Urizen, 1978); Peter Burke, *Cultura popular na idade média* (São Paulo: Companhia das Letras, 1989); and Isaiah Berlin, *The Crooked Timber of Humanity* (New York: Alfred A. Knopf, 1991). The quotations are from Elias, *Civilizing Process*, 5.

17. Bronislaw Malinowski, Introduction to *Contrapunteo cubano del tabaco y el azucar*, by Fernando Ortiz (La Habana: Editorial de Ciencias Sociales, 1991), xxxiii.

18. Hermano Vianna Jr., *O mundo funk carioca* (Rio de Janeiro: Jorge Zahar, 1988).

19. Néstor García Canclini, *Culturas híbridas* (Buenos Aires: Sudamericana, 1992), 14–15.

20. José Murilo de Carvalho, "Elite and State-Building in Imperial Brazil" (Ph.D. dissertation, Stanford University, 1975), 267–68.

21. Raimundo Faoro, *Os donos do poder* (Porto Alegre: Globo/USP, 1973), 279.

22. Carvalho, "Elite," 269.

23. Emília Viotti da Costa, *The Brazilian Empire* (Chicago: University of Chicago Press, 1985), 9.

24. Faoro, *Os donos*, 316.

25. Ludwig Lauerhass Jr., *Getúlio Vargas e o triunfo do nacionalismo brasileiro* (São Paulo: Itatiaia/Edusp, 1986), 20.

26. Ibid., 44.

27. Boris Fausto, *A revolução de 30* (São Paulo: Brasiliense, 1975), 232.

28. Octávio Ianni, *A idéia de Brasil moderno* (São Paulo: Brasiliense, 1992), 128.

29. Fausto, *Revolução*, 239–46.

30. Lauerhass, *Getúlio Vargas*, 95.

31. Carlos Guilherme Motta, *Ideologia de la cultura brasileira* (São Paulo: Atica, 1980), 58.

32. Lúcia Lippi de Oliveira, *A questão nacional na primeira república* (São Paulo: Brasiliense, 1990), 197.

CHAPTER FIVE

1. Lília Schwarcz, " 'Homens de sciencia' e a raça dos homens" (doctoral thesis, Universidad de São Paulo, 1992), 7, 12.

2. Ibid., 17.

3. Ibid., 42.

4. Ibid., 17.

5. Cited in Tzvetan Todorov, *Nós e os outros* (Rio de Janeiro: Jorge Zahar, 1993), 146.

6. Ibid., 150.

7. Graça Aranha, *Canaã* (1901; reprint, Rio de Janeiro: Ediouro, n.d.), 32.

8. Ibid., 24.

9. Ibid., 129–30.

10. José Paulo Paes, *Canaã e o ideário modernista* (São Paulo: Edusp, 1992), 93.

11. Ibid., 98.

12. For a summary of ideas on eugenics, see Schwarcz "Homens," esp. 61–62. On the Brazilian national polemic over them, see Dante Moreira Leite, *O carácter nacional brasileiro* (São Paulo: Pioneira, 1976), and Roberto Ventura, *Estilo tropical* (São Paulo: Companhia das Letras, 1991).

13. Thales de Azevedo, "Gilberto Freyre e a reinterpretação do mestiço," in *Gilberto Freyre: Sua ciência, sua filosofia, sua arte* (Rio de Janeiro: José Olympio, 1962), 74.

14. Sílvio Romero, "Sílvio Romero," in *Caminhos do pensamento crítico* (Rio de Janeiro: Pallas/MEC, 1972), 435.

15. Ibid., 436.

16. Ventura, *Estilo*, 51.

17. Ibid., 51.

18. Quoted in Leite, *O carácter*, 186.

19. Freyre dedicated his book *Brasis, Brasil, Brasília* (Lisboa: Livros do Brasil, n.d.), to Lacerda, saying in the dedication that Lacerda was "the first man of science, not only in Brazil but in all America, to suggest . . . in 1911 . . . Brazil's possible contribution to solving the problem of relations between different races and civilizations."

20. Maria Laura Cavalcanti et al., "Os estudos de folclore no Brasil," in *Seminário folclore e cultura popular* (Rio de Janeiro: IBAC, 1992), 107.

21. It should be noted that Alencar sought Brazilian authenticity in other places as well. "It is in our popular song," he wrote, "that one vividly feels the ingenuous soul of a nation" (José de Alencar, "José de Alencar," in Afrânio Coutinho, *Caminhos do pensamento crítico* (Rio de Janeiro: Pallas/MEC, 1972), 168).

22. Leite, *O carácter*, 173.

23. Alfredo Bosi, *Dialectica da colonização* (São Paulo: Companhia das Letras, 1992), 179.

24. Romero, "Sílvio Romero," 469.

25. Quoted in Leite, *O carácter*, 174.

26. Romero, "Sílvio Romero," 470.

27. Ibid., 463.

28. Leite, *O carácter*, 198.

29. Ibid., 218, 230, 238, and 254.

30. Gilberto Freyre, *Ordem e progresso*, 3rd ed. (Rio de Janeiro: José Olympio, 1974), clx.

31. Giralda Seyferth, "Os paradoxos da miscigenaçãon," *Estudos Afro-Asiáticos* 20 (January 1991): 165–75.

32. Ibid., 167, 173.

33. Manuel Diégues Jr., *Inmigração, urbanização, industrialização* (Rio de Janeiro: Funarte, 1980), 335–36.

34. Seyferth, "Os paradoxos," 171.

CHAPTER SIX

1. Jorge Amado, "Casa grande e senzala e a revolução cultural," in *Gilberto Freyre: Sua ciência, sua filosofia, sua arte* (Rio de Janeiro: José Olympio, 1962), 31.

2. Ibid., 35.

3. Monteiro Lobato, "Prefácio ao *Gilberto Freyre* de Diego de Melo Menezes," in *Prefácios e entrevistas* (São Paulo: Brasiliense, 1951), 106.

4. Antônio Cândido, *O significado de* [preface of] *Raízes do Brasil*, 24th ed., by Sérgio Buarque de Holanda (Rio de Janeiro: José Olympio, 1982), xxxix-xl.

5. Thales de Azevedo, "Gilberto Freyre e a reiterpretação do mestiço," in *Gilberto Freyre*, 76–77.

6. Roberto da Matta, "A hora e a vez de Gilberto Freyre," *Folha de São Paulo*, Folhetim, 24 July 1987, B-4/B-5

7. See Bruno Latour, *The Pasteurization of France* (Cambridge: Harvard University Press, 1988).

8. Ibid., 16.

9. Freyre's biographer, relative, and "sort of secretary" Diego de Melo Menezes writes that Freyre may have been the first to use the term *miscigenação* in Brazil (Diego de Melo Menezes, *Gilberto Freyre* [Rio de Janeiro: Casa do Estudante, 1944], 167).

10. Translator's note: The term *cafuzo* describes a person of mixed African and indigenous American descent.

11. Gilberto Freyre, *Casa grande e senzala*, 21st ed. (Rio de Janeiro: José Olympio, 1981), lvii.

12. Ibid.

13. Ricardo Benzaquem de Araujo, "Guerra e paz" (doctoral thesis, PPGAS, Museu Nacional, UFRJ, 1993), 12.

14. Gilberto Freyre, *Tempo morto e outros tempos* (Rio de Janeiro: José Olympio, 1975), 68. In a letter to Oliveira Lima—dated 17 January 1921, just half a year after his arrival in New York—Freyre gives an even drier version of the event: "Today I was in Brooklyn and popped down to the 'Minas,' still under repair down at the shipyard. It anchored here in August" (Gilberto Freyre, *Cartas do próprio punho sobre pessoas e coisas do Brasil e do estrangeiro* [Brasilia: MEC, 1978] 172).

15. Freyre, *Tempo morto*, 43, 44, 62.

16. *Geografia do nordeste da Bahia* and *A pororoca do Amazonas e geologia do Brasil*.

17. Freyre, *Tempo morto*, 4.

18. Ibid., 128.

19. Ibid., 135.

20. Gilberto Freyre, "Complexidade de antropologia e complexidade do Brasil como problema antropológico," in *Problemas brasileiros de antropologia*, 3rd ed. (Rio de Janeiro: José Olympio, 1962), 34, 39.

21. Gilberto Freyre, "Continente e Ilha," in ibid., 150–51.

22. Gilberto Freyre, *Manifesto regionalista*, 4th ed. (Recife: Instituto Joaquim Nabuco, 1967), xvii, xx, xvi.

23. Ibid., 66.

24. Ibid., 67.

25. Freyre, *Tempo morto*, 45.

26. Quoted in Menezes, *Gilberto Freyre*, 84.

27. Freyre, *Tempo morto*, 221.

28. See, for example, Theodor Adorno and Max Horkheimer, "A indústria

cultural: O ilusionismo como mistifição de massa," in *Teoria da cultura da massa*, edited by Luís C. Lima (Rio de Janeiro: Paz e Terra, 1978), 105–27.

29. Gilberto Freyre, *Tempo de aprendiz*, 2 vols. (São Paulo and Brasília: Ibrasa/INL, 1979), 1:155.

30. Ibid., 257.

31. Ibid., 156.

32. Gilberto Freyre, *Sobrados e mocambos*, 4th ed. (Rio de Janeiro: José Olympio, 1968), 522.

33. Afonso Arinos, "A unidade da pátria," in *Obra completa* (Rio de Janeiro: Conselho Federal de Cultura, 1969), 895.

34. Menezes, *Gilberto Freyre*, 237.

35. Araujo, "Guerra e paz," 38.

36. Freyre, *Tempo de aprendiz*, 1:329.

37. Ibid., 70–71.

38. Araujo, "Guerra e paz," 176.

39. Ibid., 203.

40. Gilberto Freyre, *Vida, forma e cor* (Rio de Janeiro: Record, 1987), 40.

41. Ibid., 43.

42. Gilberto Freyre, *Uma cultura ameaçada: A luso-brasileira* (Rio de Janeiro: Casa do Estudante do Brasil, 1942), 26–27.

43. Freyre, *Casa grande*, 151.

44. Freyre, *Sobrados e mocambos*, 522.

CHAPTER SEVEN

1. Gilberto Freyre, *Tempo de aprendiz*, 2 vols. (São Paulo and Brasília: Ibrasa/INL, 1979), 1:329.

2. Eduardo Jardim de Moraes, *A brasilidade modernista* (Rio de Janeiro: Graal, 1978), 49.

3. Testimony cited in Blaise Cendrars, *Ouvres completes*, vol. 15 (Paris: Denoel, 1957), ix.

4. Mário da Silva Brito, *História do modernismo brasileiro* (Rio de Janeiro: Civilização Brasileira, 1974), 137.

5. For example, the modernists Oswald de Andrade and Menotti del Picchia, together with Monteiro Lobato, were invited by Washington Luís to form an official commission that would design a monument to the *bandeirantes* for the centenary of independence in 1922. São Paulo newspapers supported their design, though the gigantic (and quite modern) statue was never built. (See Brito, *História do modernismo brasileiro*, 122–27).

6. Nicolau Sevcenko, *Orfeu extático na metrópole* (São Paulo: Companhia das Letras, 1992), 247.
7. Ibid., 241.
8. Ibid., 242. The intellectual nativist current had been represented prin cipally by the *Revista do Brasil* (founded in 1916 by the Nationalist League) and by the "caipira" regionalist literature of Monteiro Lobato, Valdomiro Silveira, and Amadeu Amaral (member of the Nationalist League, contributor to the *Revista do Brasil*, and early promotor of Bra zilian folklore studies), among others.
9. Sevcenko, *Orfeu extático*, 250.
10. Cited in Brito, *História do modernismo brasileiro*, 35.
11. Benedito Nunes, "A antropofagia ao alcance de todos," in *Obras com pletas*, by Oswald de Andrade, vol. 6 (Rio de Janeiro: Civilização Brasi leira, 1978), xviii.
12. Cendrars, *Ouvres completes*, viii.
13. Blaise Cendrars, *Etc. . . . etc. . . . : Um livro 100% brasileiro* (São Paulo: Prespectiva, 1976), 35.
14. Sevcenko, *Orfeu extático*, 288.
15. James Clifford, *The Predicament of Culture* (Cambridge: Harvard Univer sity Press, 1988), 197. Sevcenko provides a more complex description of Picasso's approach to African art, noting that the painter was not really seeking "the authenticity of the primitive, the truth of forms, the spontaneity of the unconscious, original purity, or anything of the sort." See Sevcenko, *Orfeu extático*, 195–97.
16. Clifford, *Predicament of Culture*, 200.
17. From French: "des 1919, l'art africain entre, progressivement, dans le domaine public et dans le circuit commercial, et devient perie inte grante du pantheon esthetique" (Jean Laude, *La peinture française* [1905–1914] *et l'"arte nègre"* [Paris: Klincksieck, 1968], 11).
18. Cendrars mentioned these unrealized plans in an interview with French radio, apropos of his admiration for the nineteenth-century Brazilian poet Gregório de Matos. Blaise Cendrars, *Blaise Cendrars vous parle* (Paris: Denoel, 1952), 66, 67.
19. See "Blaise Cendrars," in the *Glossário de homens e coisas da Estética* (1924/1925), xxiv.
20. Cendrars, *Blaise Cendrars*, 68–69.
21. From an account by the journalist Brito Broca, first published in 1960 by the *Gazeta* of São Paulo, quoted in Aracy de Amaral, *Blaise Cendrars no Brasil e os modernistas* (São Paulo: Martin Fontes, 1968), 42–43.
22. Cendrars, *Blaise Cendrars*, 72–73.
23. Ibid., 73.

24. Vasco Mariz, *Heitor Villa-Lobos* (Belo Horizonte: Itatiaia, 1989), 50.

25. From his autobiographical *Notes sans musique* (1945), quoted in "Darius Milhaud," *Enciclopédia de música brasileira.*

26. Sevcenko, *Orfeu extático*, 278.

27. Nunes, "Antropofagia," xxxiii.

28. Mário de Andrade, *Ensaio sobre a música brasileira* (São Paulo: Martins, 1962), 17.

29. Ibid., 15.

30. Ibid., 14.

31. Ibid., 16.

32. Ibid., 29.

33. Quoted in Eduardo Jardim de Moraes, "Modernismo e folclore," in *Seminário folclore e cultura popular* (Rio de Janeiro: IBAC, 1992), 77.

34. Mário de Andrade, "A música e a canção populares no Brasil," n.p., 1936, 4. (Typescript housed in the Biblioteca Nacional, Rio.)

35. Article first published in *O estado de Pará* (22 July 1928), later made into a chapter in *Essay on Brazilian Music*, 126.

36. Andrade, *Ensaio*, 126.

37. Sevcenko, *Orfeu extático*, 300.

CHAPTER EIGHT

1. The founding of the station was the initiative of Henrique Morize, a scientist, and of Roquette Pinto, an anthropologist who, several years later, defended the Brazilian mestiço against Arianist criticisms at the Brazilian Eugenics Congress of 1929. Gilberto Freyre, *Casa grande e senzala*, 21st ed. (Rio de Janeiro: José Olympio, 1981), Preface to 1st ed.

2. The idea appears in his 1 May 1937 message to the Brazilian Congress, quoted in Sérgio Cabral, "Getúlio Vargas e a música popular brasileira," in *Ensaios de opiniao* 2:36–41.

3. On early Brazilian radio, see José Ramos Tinhorão, *Música popular: Do gramofone ao rádio e tv* (São Paulo: Atica, 1981); Sérgio Cabral, *No tempo de Almirante* (Rio de Janeiro: Francisco Alves, 1990); and Almirante, *No tempo de Noel Rosa* (Rio de Janeiro: Francisco Alves, 1977), 30–36.

4. From the newspaper *Pasquim*, quoted in Lupiscínio Rodrigues, "Entrevista," in *O som do Pasquim* (Rio de Janeiro: Codecri, 1976), 68.

5. Though most of those who gathered at Aunt Ciata's house were black, not all were. Ari Vasconcelos points out that one of the musicians frequently present was Saudade, a gypsy. Vasconcelos argues that gypsies had an important secondary role in the invention of Brazil's national rhythm: "Pixinguinha and João da Bahiana revealed to me that there was a group of gypsy composers, singers, and musicians who culti-

vated samba with true mastery and who made an important, possibly decisive, contribution to the genre" (Ari Vasconcelos, "Tem cigano no samba," *Piracema* 1 (1993): 108). This information not only reaffirms the importance of Laurindo Rabelo's ethnicity in the history of Brazilian popular music. It also further complicates the intricate network of transcultural mediations involved in "nationalizing" samba. For more on Aunt Ciata, see Roberto Moura, *Tia Ciata e a pequena África do Rio de Janeiro* (Rio de Janeiro: Funarte, 1983).

6. Enough controversy surrounds "Pelo telefone" without entering into disputes over whether other songs, like "A viola" by Catulo da Paixão Cearense (recorded a few years earlier in 1914), might better deserve the title of "first samba."

7. An interview recorded with Donga, "Transcrição datilografada de seu depoimento para o Museu da Imagem e do Som," Rio de Janeiro: gravado em 04/02/1969, 16.

8. An interview recorded with João da Bahiana, "Depoimento para o Museu da Imagem e do Som," Rio de Janeiro, gravado em 08/24/1966, 7.

9. Almirante, *No tempo de Noel Rosa*, 29.

10. Sérgio Cabral, *Pixinguinha: Vida e obra* (Rio de Janeiro: Funarte, 1978), 30.

11. Quoted in Marília Silva and Arthur Oliveira Filho, *Filho de Ogum Bexiguento* (Rio de Janeiro: Funarte, 1979), 39.

12. Ibid., 44–45.

13. See Ibid.

14. Donga, "Transcrição datilografada," 19.

15. Guinle sponsored, among other activities, the Fluminense Football Club (having even given the inauguration speech at the team's clubhouse on 18 November 1920). He also received a homage from the sambista "king" Sinhô, who dedicated a batuque to Guinle and Villa-Lobos (Jota Efegê, *Figura e coisas da música popular brasileira*, 2 vols. [Rio de Janeiro: Funarte, 1980], 2:123).

16. Donga "Transcrição datilografada," 18.

17. Quoted in Cabral, *Pixinguinha*, 37.

18. José Ramos Tinhorão, in *Música popular: Um tema em debate* (Rio de Janeiro: JCM, n.d.), 47, affirms that "the black and mestiço people of Rio went to gafiera-type dances, held in big old converted houses in the city center, Catete, or Botafogo, where—according to Jota Efegê in his book, *O cabrocha*—around 1930, 'jazz bands' also played sambas, maxixes, fox-blues, and waltzes.".

19. The other Batuta (also present at the Catete Street encounter of 1926) was Sebastião Cirino. Cirino lived fourteen years in Paris, and during

those years he gave guitar lessons to Princess Maria Thereza of the former Brazilian royal family. Whatever stigma was once attached to the lowly guitar had obviously evaporated in the early twentieth century (Efegê, *Figura e coisas*, 1:239).

20. Quoted in Cabral, *Pixinguinha*, 57.

21. María Laura Cavalcanti, "Onde a cidade se encontra: O desfile das escolas de samba no Rio de Janeiro" (doctoral thesis, PPGAS, Museu Nacional, UFRJ, 1993).

22. From an article first published in Sã Paulo's *Diário Nacional* after Sinhô's death in 1930: Manuel Bandeira, "O enterro de Sinhô," in *Crônicas da província do Brasil* (Rio de Janeiro: Civilizção Brasileira, 1937), 108.

23. Bandeira, "Enterro," 108.

24. Manuel Bandeira, "Sambistas," in *Crônicas da província*, 169.

25. Bandeira, "Enterro," 110.

26. The samba was "Que vale a nota sem o carinho da mulher" — see the article on "Mário Reis" in the *Enciclopédia de música brasileira*. At the time, Sinhô had several hits and was known basically as a sambista, although he had also recorded waltzes, fox-trots, Charlestons, toadas, cateretês, cocos, maxixes, and fados (Edigar de Alencar, *Nosso Sinhô do samba* [Rio de Janeiro: Funarte, 1981]).

27. See Almirante, *No tempo de Noel Rosa*, 30–36.

28. Ibid., 42.

29. Quoted in ibid., 44.

30. The lyrics quoted are from the samba *Façanha do Bando*. The first samba recorded with batucada was *Na Pavuna* (ibid., 68).

31. João Máximo and Carlos Didier, *Noel Rosa* (Brasília: UNB/linha Gráfica, 1990), 204.

32. Tinhorão, *Música popular: Um tema em debate*, 43.

33. Ibid., 47.

34. Tracing the line of evolution that comes from batuque in Angola and the Congo to *partido-alto* (a particular variant of samba de morro) we find: a) first lundu as it was danced, giving way to the lundus that were played and sung — but not danced — in the salons of the imperial period, as well as to the rural sambas of Bahia and São Paulo, to lundu variants still danced in the countryside, and to other manifestations; b) then, all these expresssions (with the *chula* of Bahian samba gaining a status apart) coming back together into what we will call the samba of "Little Africa" in Praça Onze, radiating out from the house of Tia Ciata; c) next, that samba of "Little Africa" was influenced by maxixe, giving rise to samba de morro; d) finally samba de morro split into urban samba (beginning in the neighborhood of Estácio), for singing and dancing in a parade, on the one hand, and into partido alto, for

singing in a roda (circle). Nei Lopes, O negro no Rio de Janeiro e sua tradi-
ção musical (Rio de Janeiro: Pallas, 1992), 47.

35. Sérgio Cabral, As escolas de samba (Rio de Janeiro: Fontana, 1974), 28.

36. Viola continued: "I'm surprised by all the new popular artists. It's
no longer possible to speak of samba as a timeless music. Until not
long ago, there was a samba community, but no more. There is a
young movement that wants to do things differently. The times are
changing" (Paulinho da Viola, O Globo, 10 October 1993, Segundo Caderno, 1).

37. Efegê, Figura e coisas, 1:171.

38. Tinhorão, Música popular: Um tema em debate, 82.

39. Lígia Santos and Marília Silva, Partido da portela (Rio de Janeiro: Funarte, 1980), 63.

40. Cabral, "Getúlio Vargas," 37.

41. Cláudia Matos, Acertei no milhar (Rio de Janeiro: Paz e Terra, 1982).

42. Cabral, "Getúlio Vargas," 38.

43. Efegê, Figura e coisas, 2:191.

44. Ibid., 1:63.

45. Ibid.

46. Cabral, "Getúlio Vargas," 40. Villa-Lobos had occupied an official post
in the Vargas government since 1932, as director of SEMA—Super-
intendência de Educação Musical e Artística.

47. See Mariz, Heitor Villa-Lobos, 34–35.

48. Other performers of the Caboclo house were a duo, Jacaraca and
Ratinho, formerly members of the Turunas Pernambucanos, and the
actress Dercy Gonçalves. See Sonia Rodrigues, Jararaca e ratinho (Rio de
Janeiro: Funarte, 1983).

CHAPTER NINE

1. See Antônio Risério, Caymmi: Uma utopia de lugar (São Paulo: Perspectiva, 1993), 31.

2. José Ramos Tinhorão, Música popular: Um tema em debate (Rio de Janeiro:
JCM, n.d.), 48–49.

3. José Ramos Tinhorão, Pequena história da música popular (São Paulo: Art,
1986), 231.

4. Caetano Veloso, Alegria, Alegria (Rio de Janeiro: Pedra Q Ronca, n.d.), 3.

5. Ibid., 8.

6. Ibid., 5.

7. Ibid., 23.

8. Gilberto Gil, Expresso 2222 (Salvador: Corrupio, 1982), 33.

9. Ibid., 35.

10. Ibid., 19.

11. Ibid., 23.

12. *Folha de Sã Paulo*, 24 November 1984.

13. *Jornal do Brasil*, 25 October 1983.

14. Ibid., 25 May 1985.

15. The interview was broadcast on the program "Conexão Nacional" on the Manchete television network.

16. Ibid.

17. Tinhorão, *Pequena história*, 267.

18. Antônio Risério, *Carnaval Ijexá* (Salvador: Corrupio, 1981), 31–32.

19. Rohan B. Preston, "The Olodum Movement," *New City*, 20 June 1991, 19.

20. Interview with the author, 1988.

21. *Bizz* (a Brazilian magazine devoted to pop music), May 1993.

22. Roger Wallis and Krister Malm, "Patterns of Change," in *On Record*, edited by Simon Frith and Andrew Goodwin (New York: Pantheon, 1990), 179. (In this article Wallis and Malm summarize their findings from their book *The Music Industry in Small Countries: Big Sounds from Small Peoples* [Taby, Sweden: Wassbergs Tryckeri, 1985].)

23. Wallis and Malm, "Patterns of Change." For the purposes of their research, Wallis and Malm define "transculturation" specifically as "a process whereby elements of music and technology spread by the transnational industry are incorporated into local music." The international repercussion of Jamaican reggae (whether recognized as such or disguised as common "roots") demonstrates that this is not a simple, one-way flow from the developed to the developing world.

24. *O Globo*, 8 April 1986.

CHAPTER TEN

1. At the time of this interview, proposals for the independence of several southern states had awakened a lively discussion in the Brazilian press. (*Jornal do Brasil*, 1 June 1990, B-1).

2. The song was later recorded on a disk called *Circuladô ao vivo*, Polygram, 1992.

3. See Antônio Risério, *Textos e tribos* (Rio de Janeiro: Imago, 1993), the most determined scholarly attack on this exclusion.

4. Eduardo Viveiros de Castro, "La marbre et le mytre," in *Mémoire de la tradition*, edited by A. Becquelin and A. Molinié (Nanterre: Société d'Ethnologie, 1993), 371–72.

5. Mario Vargas Llosa, "Une culture du métissage," *Magazine Littéraire* 296 (February 1992): 59.

6. Carlos Fuentes, "Nous, Ibéro-Americains," *Magazine Littéraire* 296 (February 1992): 62.

7. Jean Baudrillard, *La transparence du mal* (Paris: Galilée, 1990), 130.

8. Claude Lévi-Strauss, "Raça e história," in *Antropologia estrutural* (Rio de Janeiro: Tempo Brasileiro, 1976), 365.

9. For a basic primer on the historical development of the concept of entropy, featuring its application to information science, see Jeremy Campbell, *Grammatical Man* (New York: Simon & Schuster, 1982).

10. Francisco Guimarães, *Na roda do samba* (Rio de Janeiro: Funarte, 1978), 28.

11. Todorov, *Nós e os outros*, 14–15.

12. Gilberto Velho, *Destino: Campo de possibilidades e províncias de significado* (1989), 1.

13. Edgar Morin, "Le défi de la complexité," in *Science avec conscience* (Paris: Fayard, 1990), 168.

14. Ibid.

15. Gilles Deleuze, "Mediators," in *Incorporations*, ed. Jonathan Crary and Sanford Kwinter (New York: Zone, 1992), 285.

16. Claude Lévi-Strauss, "A estructura dos mitos," in *Antropologia estructural*, 261.

17. Freyre further augments the logical difficulties of his homogenizing project by praising "transnational regionalism" (Freyre, *Brasis, Brasil, Brasília* [Lisboa: Livros do Brasil, n.d.], 135).

18. Roberto Schwarz, "Fim de século," *Folha de São Paulo*, 4 December 1994, 6.

19. *IstoÉ*, 21 December 1994, 84.

20. Roger Bastide, *Brasil, terra de contrastes* (São Paulo: Difusão Europeia do Livro, 1973), 8.

21. Roberto da Matta, *O que faz o brasil, Brasil?* (Rio de Janeiro: Salamandra, 1984), 113.

INDEX

70; and blacks, 71; and African art, 72; and samba, 112

Frankel, Isaac, 81–82

Freyre, Gilberto: and Brazilian social thought, xvii; and mestiço nationalism, xvii, 43; samba encounter of, xviii, 1–9, 10, 13, 79, 85; and racial mixing, 2, 14, 36, 37, 43, 45, 47, 51–52, 54, 56, 62–63, 71, 126 (n. 19); on James Joyce, 5–6; and modernism, 6, 29; and regionalism, 8, 31, 41; and Afro-Brazilian culture, 8–9, 59, 109; and popular music, 14; on elites, 18; on modinha, 19–20; and re-Europeanization, 23; and tropicalism, 48–49; and Torres, 50; and cuisine, 53, 60, 70; New York diary of, 56; and cosmopolitanism, 57, 60, 62, 94–95; antiforeign attitudes of, 59; and empathy, 65; and black valorization, 67; and Jorge, 103; and Chico Science & Nação Zumbi, 105; and Veloso, 108; and homogeneity, 109, 112; and heterogeneity, 111–12; and national identity, 116

—works: *Tempo morto e outros tempos*, 1; *The Masters and the Slaves*, 2, 8, 12, 13, 41, 43, 49, 51, 53–55, 59, 66; "On the Valorization of Things Black," 8–9; "The Threatened Luso–Brazilian Culture," 51; *Civilization and Race Mixing*, 53; "The Complexity of Anthropology and the Complexity of Brazil as an Anthropological Problem," 58; *Regionalist Manifesto*, 58–59; *Apprentice Time*, 60; *The Mansions*

and the Shanties, 62, 64–66, 111–12; *Order and Progress*, 66

Fry, Peter, 11–12, 13

Fuentes, Carlos, 110

Fujita, Tzuguharu, 91

Funk music, xiv, 36, 89

Futurism, 70

Gallet, Luciano, 1

García Canclini, Néstor, 16, 36

German immigrants, 50, 63, 64, 109

Gil, Gilberto, 96, 98, 102, 107; "Roque Santeiro," 97

Gilberto, João, 93, 95

Gobineau, Joseph Arthur de, 44–46, 51

Gomes, Carlos, 19

Gonçalves, Ledo, 121 (n. 9)

Gonçalves Dias, Antônio, 20

Grupo de Caxangá, 28, 79, 82, 123 (n. 44)

Guinle, Arnaldo, 83, 131 (n. 15)

Gypsies, 20, 21, 112, 130–31 (n. 5)

Habanera, 27

Harlem Renaissance, 61

Hegemonic culture, 36

Herder, Johann Gottfried, 35

Heterogeneity, 21, 27, 35, 40, 108, 109, 111–12, 114–16

Homogeneity, 35, 41, 50, 52, 58, 108–12, 114–15, 116, 118

Hybrid cultures, 36–37

Ilê Aiyê, 100, 102

Immigrants and immigration, 39, 40, 50–51, 63

Indianism, 47–48, 68

Intellectuals: and Cendrars, 9; and popular culture, 14–15; and samba, 15; and invention of tradition, 15–16; and nationalism, 39; and national identity, 43; and racial mixing, 44, 49, 50, 54; and authenticity, 48; and Freyre, 55, 56, 60; and nativism, 129 (n. 8). *See also* Elites

Jamaica, 104, 134 (n. 23)
Japanese immigrants, 51
Jazz, 27, 60–62, 83–84, 95, 97, 131 (n. 18)
Jewish population, 63
João VI (regent of Portugal), 37–38
Jobim, Antônio Carlos, 93, 95
Jorge, João, 103
Jovem Guarda, 104
Joyce, James, 5–6, 57

Lacerda, João Batista, 47, 50, 126 (n. 19)
Lambada, 100
Levi-Strauss, Claude: *Race and History*, 111
Lima, Jorge de, 117; *Poemas negros*, 65; "A minha América," 65, 108
Lins do Rego, José, 5
Lobato, Monteiro, 53, 128 (n. 5), 129 (n. 8)
Lopes, Nei, 88, 98
Lundu, 17, 18, 19, 20, 22, 27–28, 82, 132 (n. 34)
Luso-tropicalism, 48–49, 53, 62–63, 64, 66

Machado de Assis, Joaquim Maria, 20, 30
Macumba rites, 85, 86
Malinowski, Bronislaw, 36
Malm, Krister, and Roger Wallis: *The Music Industry in Small Countries*, 104
Mambos, 28

Mangueira, 91, 107
Manuel, Francisco, 20
Manuel, Joaquim, 121 (n. 7)
Marcha, 11, 78
Mariano, Olegário, 29, 80
Marshall, Sam, 27
Martins, Wilson, 122 (n. 27)
Mass media, xviii, 19, 100, 104. *See also* Radio
The Masters and the Slaves (Freyre): and Brazilian identity, 2, 13; and Afro-Brazilian culture, 8; and racial mixing, 12, 43, 49, 51, 53; and nationalism, 41; reaction to, 53–55; *Regionalist Manifesto* compared to, 59; popular music in, 66
Masurkas, 27, 78
Maxixe, 27–28, 76, 78, 82, 88–89, 92
Medeiros, Anacleto de, 23
Meneses, Emílio de, 29
Menezes, Diego de Melo, 62, 127 (n. 9)
Mercury, Daniela, 100
Merengue, 89
Mestiçagem, xiii, 2, 36–37, 94, 111, 112, 113, 117
Mestiço culture, 54, 55, 56, 60, 106, 110, 112, 114, 116, 117
Mestiço nationalism, xv, xvii, 43, 44, 53, 75
Mestiço novel, 53
Middle class, 86–87, 88, 95, 98, 105, 114
Milhaud, Darius, 71, 73–74; "Le boeuf sur le toit," 73, 74; "Dances of Jacarémirim," 74; "Nostalgia for Brazil," 74
Miranda, Carmen, 62, 66, 91, 92, 93–94; "They Said I Came Back Americanized," 93

10, 28; as national music, xvii, 37, 41, 65, 73, 78, 84, 86, 90, 92, 94, 102, 105, 112, 114, 118; and popular culture, xviii; and national identity, 8, 10, 14–16, 49, 53, 112, 113; repression of, 10, 11–12, 81; history of, 10–16, 79; and elites, 11, 20; and trans-culturation, 36; and Freyre, 61, 62; and Luso-tropicalism, 66; evolution of, 88, 96, 106, 132 (n. 34); and national unity, 107

Samba-bolero, 95

Samba-canção, 95

Samba de morro, 88, 89–90, 95, 113

Samba de roda, 96

Samba-reggae, 102, 105, 106

Samba schools, 89, 90, 91, 92, 107, 114

Sambistas: blacks as, xiii, 6; filming of, xiii–xvi; and Freyre, 1–2, 5, 6, 7; and elites, 10, 15, 85; and national identity, 15, 94; external relation of, 16; repression of, 81, 112–13; and Sinhô's funeral, 86; and blocos afros, 102

Santo Amaro, Prisciliana de, 81

Santos, Ernesto Joaquim Maria dos. *See* Donga

Santos, Marquesa de, 19

São Paulo: and revolution of 1930, 3; and modernism, 4, 5, 68, 71, 128 (n. 5); mass media of, 100; sambas of, 132 (n. 34)

Saudade, 130–31 (n. 5)

Schottisches, 27, 78

Sertanejo music, 27, 28, 69, 78, 82, 83, 103

Sevcenko, Nicolau, 69, 129 (n. 15)

Seyferth, Giralda, 50, 51

Silva, Arnani, 91

Silva, Ismael, 11, 87; "If You Swear," 89

Silveira, Valdomiro, 129 (n. 8)

Simmel, Georg, 34, 114

Simon, Paul: *Rhythm of the Saints*, 102

Sinhô das Crioulas, 11, 23, 85–86, 131 (n. 15), 132 (n. 26)

Slaves and slavery, xiii, 7, 27, 80, 101

Son, 89

Souza, Inglês de, 50

Suingue, xiv, 102

Tangos, 28, 78

Tanguinhos, 75

Teffé, Nair de, 25

Teixeira, Patrício, 1, 2, 5, 7, 8, 92

Teixeirinha, 79

Tigre, Bastos, 29

Tinhorão, José Ramos, 18, 19, 24, 27, 87–88, 95, 98

Tinoco, 23

Todorov, Tzvetan, 44–45, 114

Torres, Alberto, 39, 50

Transculturation, 36–37, 74, 80, 103–5, 114, 134 (n. 23)

Trios eléctricos, 100–101, 103–4

Tropicalism, 12, 48–49, 96–99, 107

Trovador, Alexandre, 22

Turunas da Mauricéia, 86

Turunas Pernambucanos, 57, 86

United States: popular music from, xiv, 27, 94; influence on Brazil, xvii, 38; and Freyre, 1, 55, 61; and racial attitudes, 13, 14; and country music, 15–16; funk music of, 36; black poetry in, 65; and cultural imperialism, 84; and Miranda, 93; and blocos afros, 101; and Olodum, 102–3; and multiracialism, 118

Urban Brazilians: and United States' music, 36; and national identity, 49, 65; and popular music, 76, 78, 83, 88; and rock music, 98

Vargas, Alzira, 92
Vargas, Getúlio, 40, 51, 77, 90–92
Vargas Llosa, Mario, 110
Vasconcelos, Ari, 130–31 (n. 5)
Velho, Gilberto, 21, 88, 114
Velloso, Mônica, 23

Veloso, Caetano, 95–96, 107–8, 117; "Americanos," 108
Villa-Lobos, Heitor, 1, 7–8, 24, 66, **73**, 91, 92
Viola, Paulinho da, 89, 106, 133 (n. 36)
Viveiros de Castro, Eduardo, 110

Wallerstein, Immanuel, 33–34
Wallis, Roger, and Krister Malm: *The Music Industry in Small Countries*, 104
Waltzes, 27, 28, 78

Young Guard, 104

CPSIA information can be obtained at www.ICGtesting.com
Printed in the USA
BVOW011801121212

307978BV00003B/416/A